What Your Colleagues Are Saying . . .

"Finally! A book with more light than heat on the issues surrounding the standards and their implications for learning. This is a well-argued, even-handed, and clear-headed look at the need to distinguish the value of the Common Core State Standards from some of the questionable views of teaching and learning that Standards writers and promoters have been expressing. . . . Every teacher of reading, supervisor, and district leader will find value in this text."

—GRANT WIGGINS, Coauthor of *Understanding by Design*

"This book represents what we should all be doing with the CCSS—making suggestions for modifying them so that they stand a chance of achieving the goals behind them. Unless the CCSS are a living document that can be shaped and reshaped by the educators and students who are held accountable to them, they will fail. Read this book to help them succeed."

—P. DAVID PEARSON, Professor of the Graduate School of Education, University of California, Berkeley

"Talk about overdue! This book is an urgently needed corrective to the oversights, overreaches, and idiosyncratic weirdness of the Common Core State Standards and what their authors say about how they should be taught. These authors aren't Standards-bashing; they stipulate that the Common Core has 'the capacity to provide a real opportunity for progressive change.' . . . Thank goodness three of our best teacher-thinkers have come forward to speak truth to zombie literacy."

—HARVEY "SMOKEY" DANIELS, Coauthor of *The Best-Kept Teaching Secret*

"Michael Smith, Deborah Appleman, and Jeff Wilhelm seek to salvage the Common Core State Standards from both their friends and their enemies. On the one hand, they systematically debunk the destructive pedagogy that many friends of the Standards have advocated. . . . On the other hand, they demonstrate to those who would reject the Standards how they can enrich good practice as it has emerged from the past thirty years of research in reading and writing instruction. Readable, classroom friendly, and realistic, *Uncommon Core* is a must-read for everyone struggling with the current wave of curriculum reform."

—ARTHUR APPLEBEE, Distinguished Professor and Director, Center on English Learning & Achievement, University at Albany

"Prompted primarily by David Coleman's ill-informed interpretation of the instructional implications of the CCSS, Smith, Appleman, and Wilhelm have written an important and compelling book describing the kinds of instruction that will help teachers and students actually achieve the goals of the Common Core. With lucid descriptions and a host of classroom-tested examples, the authors demonstrate *'Where the Authors of the Standards Go Wrong About Instruction—and How You Can Get It Right.'"*

—MICHAEL F. GRAVES, University of Minnesota, Emeritus

un
common
core

For Peggy Jo Wilhelm, and her
uncommon core of courage and resilience.

Where the Authors of the Standards
Go Wrong About Instruction—
and How You Can Get It Right

un
common
core

Michael W. Smith
Deborah Appleman
Jeffrey D. Wilhelm
Foreword by Grant Wiggins

CORWIN
A SAGE Company

FOR INFORMATION:

Corwin

A SAGE Company

2455 Teller Road

Thousand Oaks, California 91320

(800) 233-9936

www.corwin.com

SAGE Publications Ltd.

1 Oliver's Yard

55 City Road

London EC1Y 1SP

United Kingdom

SAGE Publications India Pvt. Ltd.

B 1/I 1 Mohan Cooperative Industrial Area

Mathura Road, New Delhi 110 044

India

SAGE Publications Asia-Pacific Pte. Ltd.

3 Church Street

#10-04 Samsung Hub

Singapore 049483

Publisher: Lisa Luedeke

Editorial Development Manager: Julie Nemer

Editorial Assistant: Francesca Dutra Africano

Production Editor: Melanie Birdsall

Copy Editor: Linda Gray

Typesetter: C&M Digitals (P) Ltd.

Proofreader: Wendy Jo Dymond

Indexer: Molly Hall

Cover Designer: Rose Storey

Copyright © 2014 by Corwin

Common Core State Standards (CCSS) cited throughout the book are copyright © 2010 National Governors Association Center for Best Practices and Council of Chief State School Officers. All rights reserved.

Photos by Deborah Kowalchuk.

The views expressed within are those of the authors and do not reflect the opinions of Corwin, SAGE Publications, Inc., or their affiliated companies.

Printed in the United States of America

A catalog record of this book is available from the Library of Congress.

ISBN: 978-1-4833-3352-6

This book is printed on acid-free paper.

SUSTAINABLE FORESTRY INITIATIVE
Certified Chain of Custody
Promoting Sustainable Forestry
www.sfiprogram.org
SFI-01268
SFI label applies to text stock

14 15 16 17 18 10 9 8 7 6 5 4 3 2 1

Contents

List of Figures

Visit the companion website at
www.corwin.com/uncommoncore
for downloadable resources.

Foreword

///

Whither Common Core? As I write, this is a very live question. A conflu-
ence of factors has brought intense criticism—some of it substantive,
some of it political—on the provenance, process, and implementation
of the Standards. So, while the idea of national standards remains a
sound one, as the authors here note, the devil is in the implementation
details. And ironically (given the emphasis on the aim of dispassionate
argument in the Standards), polemics are currently drowning out sound
reasoning.

That is why Michael, Deborah, and Jeff have done the profession a great
service in this book. Finally! A text with more light than heat on the
issues surrounding the Standards and their implications for learning. We
come to understand through their clear and well-documented analysis
precisely what the Standards do and do not imply for practice, and we
gain endless practical advice on how to use the Standards to make intel-
ligent progress in literacy development.

With regard to dispassionate argument, the authors provide readers with
a fair and helpful account of the ebb and flow of views about reading
over the past 75 years and how those views have played into the English
language arts (ELA) Standards. Here, for example, are the authors lament-
ing how the important advance of reader-response theory nonetheless
led to excess (see pages 29–30):

> Lois Tyson (2006) reminds us that "the New Critics believed
> that the timeless meaning of the text—what the text is—is
> contained in the text alone" (p. 170). Reader-response critics
> contend that "what a text is cannot be separated from what it
> does" (p. 170). The role of the reader, then, and how he or she

responds to any particular text, cannot be separated from our
understanding of the text itself. . . .

Yet in some ways, as a profession, we overcorrected. In some
cases we threw the text out with the bathwater, leaving some
pretty sloppy practices that encourage personal revelation at the
expense of textual interpretation. . . . As English teachers, we
may have been guilty of overprivileging and romanticizing the
individual at the expense of considerations of context and text.

But their even-handed history is merely a backdrop for a forceful argument as to what kind of instruction best supports the Standards. The
authors clearly show how close reading—a performance at the heart
of the Standards—is helped, not hurt, by the appropriate use of valid
comprehension strategies and reader-response activities that involve
pre-reading questions, discussions, and surveys that assist in meaning making. Why is this important? Because the chief author of the
Standards—David Coleman—has spoken out against such practices
(even as he acknowledges his limited experience in teaching and with
the research on literacy).

The authors are most astute in showing that Coleman's constant emphasis on text-dependent questions actually undercuts the aim of transfer—a
goal that Coleman, the authors, and I all agree is crucial while too rarely
achieved. The authors effectively marshal the evidence as well as common sense to show that burying one's nose in each text, in isolation, is
highly unlikely to foster the kind of strategic thinking and connections
across texts that transfer requires—to the additional detriment of likely
decreases in student engagement.

They remind us that transfer demands metacognition and the ability to
(consciously) apply powerful strategies to new texts:

What research on transfer teaches us is that students must
have conscious control over what they will transfer and plenty
of practice in doing so. Research on classroom discourse
teaches us that the asking of authentic questions that foster
open discussion among students, discussions in which they

can hear and evaluate multiple interpretations, is associated
with improved performance on complex literacy tasks.

What makes the book a must-have for every teacher is that the authors
never rest content in merely making these kinds of academic arguments. Each chapter is filled with clear, practical, and rich examples
for how teachers might honor "best practice" while also meeting the
Standards. In each chapter we see best practice modeled and discussed
in a way that will help all teachers, novice and veteran, be more effective
teachers of reading.

In sum, this is a book that represents the best in teacher education and
professional development: a seamless melding of theory and practice,
argument, and advice. The book practices what the writing standards
preach and helps us experience directly what the reading standards
demand. In short: an anchor text for the anchor standards.

—Grant Wiggins

Grant Wiggins is the president of Authentic Education and the author
of numerous books and articles on curriculum and assessment. He is
perhaps best known for being the coauthor of *Understanding by Design*.

Acknowledgments

There are of course so many people, teachers all, who have helped us on our own human journeys, our educational journeys, and our specific journey writing this book. But here we would like to focus on just two acknowledgments. The rest of you know who you are and have our gratitude and love.

First, we'd like to thank Lisa Luedeke, Maura Sullivan, Francesca Africano, Melanie Birdsall, Julie Nemer, Linda Gray, and the whole team at Corwin. They have been delightful to work with, and their expertise and passion have made lots of things better, including us as writers and the book you hold in your hands.

Second, we have dedicated this book to Peggy Jo Wilhelm, Jeff's wife and a teacher extraordinaire. We'd like to explain why.

Seven years ago Peggy collapsed of a massive cerebral hemorrhage. In the intervening years she was told that she was terminal on four occasions. She has suffered 17 more strokes, all resulting in traumatic brain injury, and has lost her vision and ability to read and play music (she was a professional musician and a music and humanities teacher).

Throughout all of this, she retained her amazing grace and courage, and, perhaps most inspiring, remained a teacher. She has worked with the Healthwise project to educate legislators and the public about patients' issues when moving between doctors and hospitals, about abuses from health insurance companies, about the effects of undiagnosed diseases, and much more. She has also continued to be a guest teacher in classrooms of all kinds regarding her own condition, but also about many other topics in the arts and human psychology. She is a prized thinking partner of Boise State Writing Project teachers who invite her into their classrooms whenever she feels well enough to come. She is a model of service and of service learning.

Suffice to say that beyond the very worthy goals of teaching our students to become career and college ready, to become lifelong readers and writers, and to become democratic citizens, we want to help our students to become teachers, thinking partners, helpmates and companions to all around them, to become wide-awake and committed citizens, and to become compassionate and loving human beings. We want to help them become full human beings, even in the greatest distress. We want them to become like Peggy Jo Wilhelm.

The Promise and the Peril of the Common Core State Standards

1

After a recent talk, one of us was talking to a state's English Language Arts Coordinator. Her state had dropped writing from its exam because of the expense of scoring it, and so teachers had, she said, stopped teaching it. "The Common Core State Standards will do so much for the kids of this state. They'll finally get to write again." And she continued with a story about how much her fourth-grade daughter was enjoying having the chance to express herself in the writing she was doing in class.

But we're worried about other possible stories. Imagine an average-track 11th-grade classroom in which students are asked to read the first paragraph of Emerson's "Society and Solitude," one of the exemplar texts in Appendix B of the Common Core State Standards (CCSS) document (National Governors Association Center for Best Practices/Council of Chief State School Officers [NGA Center/CCSSO], 2010b). Here are the first two sentences they'd encounter:

> I fell in with a humorist on my travels, who had in his chamber a cast of the Rondanini Medusa, and who assured me that the name which that fine work of art bore in the

//

We think that the
Common Core
Standards have the
capacity to provide
a real opportunity
for progressive
change in American
education.

catalogues was a misnomer, as he was convinced that the
sculptor who carved it intended it for Memory, the mother of
the Muses. In the conversation that followed, my new friend
made some extraordinary confessions. "Do you not see," he
said, "the penalty of learning, and that each of these scholars
whom you have met at S—, though he were to be the last
man, would, like the executioner in Hood's poem, guillotine
the last but one?"

What do you see in your mind's eye? We see heads on desks. Shuffling
feet. Eyes darting to the teacher, silently asking for help that's not
forthcoming.

Imagine the teacher of class the night before, preparing a list of questions to ask about that text. Maybe "What does the humorist mean by
saying that the name of the Rondanini Medusa is a misnomer? What
does Emerson accomplish by beginning with that little story?" The
questions would be met with silence, we fear, and would be followed by
the temptation for the teacher to answer them himself or herself.

Imagine facing a week of such discussions, as five days were allotted for
discussion of the essay in the pacing guide. Imagine getting a note from
the department secretary saying that classroom copies of the next text to
be read in class, G. K. Chesterton's "The Fallacy of Success" (the next one
in line in the informational text list for 11th graders) were now ready.
Imagine taking that text home to prepare another set of questions to be
greeted by another round of silence.

The CCSS is coming under a lot of critique these days. Criticizing it
seems *de rigueur* and there seems to be a *critique du jour*. We might be
accused of piling on the usual heap of criticism with this current vol-
ume. But we think not. In fact, although we each have different attitudes toward the CCSS, we think that they have the capacity to provide
a real opportunity for progressive change in American education.

But we worry about what the CCSS leave out. We worry about how they
might be used in schools. And we worry even more about some of the
instructional ideas promulgated by authors of the Standards, ideas that
are, research tells us, just plain wrong-headed and misinformed, ideas
that are likely to undermine the good that the CCSS could potentially

do for the profession of teaching and for the enhanced engagement and learning of students. The purpose of this book is to speak out against those ideas and to suggest alternative instructional ideas that will better achieve the promise of the Standards.

Whenever we write anything, either alone or together, we have the goal that the work will become archival—in other words, that it will become something that needs to be contended with over time. That goal poses a problem in this particular case, since we are writing about a current issue that is taking place at a particular historical moment.

In brainstorming about the book, Jeff wrote this e-mail to Michael and Deborah:

> My big worry is that I want the book to become archival, so I want it to be about really substantive issues and thinking and principles that are important over time, and not just about the CCSS, though I know the CCSS is the immediate lever for writing the book. I think this would be possible to do.

Michael and Deborah immediately jumped in and agreed that we would foreground ideas that are salient in the research base about instructional practice and learning, that are important and even liberating for teachers to think about, and that have a very real positive impact on students—things worth thinking about in this historical moment but also well beyond it.

Here we go!

What's to Like About the CCSS

It's powerful to have shared understandings.

And it's good to be clear about these understandings. Good reading, communicative composing, facility with speaking and listening, and powerful and correct language use don't change with localities. As Grant Wiggins (2013) has put it,

> There's no Virginia algebra or Nebraska reading. There is little disagreement about what constitutes good outcomes in reading, writing and math, yet by allowing the states to define

those outcomes, place them willy-nilly in different grades, and test for them idiosyncratically we put students in a mobile society at a great disadvantage.

When instruction is centered on common goals, then it becomes easier for teachers to share their thinking and their practices. Common goals allow teachers to work together and to discuss how best to achieve those goals grade by grade and discipline by discipline. For example, in one district that we know, the teachers have agreed both on a general rubric they will use for all writing assignments and on a specific one for argument. Though these rubrics are modified grade by grade, every teacher in every subject has committed to teaching and evaluating writing in terms of the CCSS as they are reflected in the school's rubric. We're confident that this district is going to produce better writing than they have in the past and that students are going to develop clear ideas about what constitutes quality writing and quality argumentation.

What happens within schools can happen across schools as well. The CCSS are already bringing an explosion of resources for teachers that can be shared by all teachers. These resources won't just be commercial—they will be produced by teachers for other teachers and will be revised by those teachers to meet the needs of their own classroom. One of the criteria of a profession is that it creates its own knowledge, then develops and monitors its own expertise. The CCSS provide a chance for teaching to become more professionalized.

As Wiggins (2013) points out, consistency across schools also benefits students. Ours is a highly mobile society, and as Wiggins explains, "To have everyone in the country studying the same subject at the same time makes it easier for families to cope with school changes."

The CCSS provide focus: They are few in number and vertically aligned and applied across disciplines.

Our own experience working in schools is that there always seem to be 27 competing initiatives going on at once. As a result, nothing of substantive and lasting import ever really seems to get done. The CCSS provide a potential remedy for this. They are few in number and vertically aligned. They apply across disciplines, so every teacher at every grade in every content area will be working toward the same goals. Imagine what could happen with that kind of powerful and shared focus.

As English teachers, we know what it's like to have the sole burden placed on us for teaching reading, writing, speaking, and listening. The CCSS call for this responsibility to be shared across all teachers, making it ever more likely that our students will get the assistance and practice that they need to become highly literate. Also, we know that reading and writing in science is different from reading and writing in English language arts (ELA). Scientists, for example, read and write particular kinds of texts that are built on particular kinds of data. What constitutes evidence and reasoning in a scientific argument is different than it is in the humanities. So we really need all content area teachers to be on board in teaching their students how to read and write and think and problem solve like scientists—or social scientists, mathematicians, and the like.

The CCSS emphasizes process and strategies.

One of the elements of the CCSS that immediately impressed us was the focus on processes and strategies. (We'll see in subsequent chapters how this focus on processes and strategies doesn't jibe with some of the instructional suggestions made by authors of the Standards.) One of us recently spoke at a conference right after a futurist. This futurist maintained that in our rapidly changing world, available information doubles every six to seven months. Seventy percent of today's kindergartners will work in careers that don't currently exist or will be radically reconfigured, are not of thought of yet, or are not thought of in their current form.

Our students will have to solve problems that as yet have no solutions and will have to deal with problems that have not yet emerged. What good is static information in a world like this? What our students will need to develop is a problem-solving stance and the capacity to read, write, think, learn, and inquire. What they need is the ability to solve the new problems they will face.

We also like how the CCSS focus on higher-order thinking and on understanding and use. If you look, for example, at reading Anchor Standard 1 you will see that it says, "Read closely to determine what the text says explicitly and to make logical inferences from it; cite specific textual evidence when writing or speaking to support conclusions drawn from the text." Notice that the first clause indicates literal comprehension, but everything else is about inferring and evidentiary reasoning. The rest of the reading standards are all about higher-order thinking, and the CCSS make it clear that literal comprehension is not a goal in itself but is in service of the higher-order processes that depend on it.

The CCSS can promote professionalization of teaching/ encouragement of creativity and knowledge making.

A lot of teachers we know are going crazy about the CCSS and the new testing regime that will follow. We really don't see anything in the Standards themselves or on the sample review test items for PARCC (Partnership for Assessment of Readiness for College and Careers) or Smarter Balanced Tests that would require slavish test preparation. In fact, the tests won't test recall of information since they will provide all the information or provide time for students to gather their own. The tests are being designed to actually provide feedback about student mastery of the higher-order strategies in the Core.

As Wiggins (2013) writes, "The standards are like building code. It is foolish to argue that building code inhibits the architect from creating a beautiful and functional dwelling. Yet, there is a lot of hysterical talk now about just such inhibition." To think that the Standards will constrain curriculum, we think, is to misread them, and to think that we will need to teach to the test is both a misunderstanding and a failure of imagination. As you'll see in the rest of this book, we want to think hard about the possibilities that the CCSS open up for both teachers and students. Far from limiting or dumbing down teaching, we think the CCSS can invigorate and enliven teaching and discussions about teaching because, in our view, the evidence is clear that sociocultural models of teaching, particularly inquiry models, are the best way to achieve those Standards. Having long been proponents for inquiry-oriented instruction, we're excited that the CCSS could provide a lever for promoting this kind of progressive instruction.

However, we have to recognize that the emphasis on high-stakes standardized tests that has accompanied the CCSS militates against the professionalization of teachers. The continued outsourcing of assessment comes at a time when there is robust and growing evidence from the research community that frequent, high-quality *classroom assessment* produces achievement gains that far exceed those of any other single intervention strategy.

To quote Paul Zavitovsky (2012),

> "'Inside the Black Box' [see Black & William, 1998], the now-classic study of classroom assessment practices, reported strong academic gains when frequent, high-quality classroom assessment, particularly formative assessment, was practiced. At the top end of the range, these gains were roughly equivalent to the difference between overall averages on state and national tests, and the averages posted by our lowest-achieving schools.

> Given what we know about the culture of American teaching and the power of high-quality classroom assessment, the troubling thing about current work on Common Core assessment is that we seem to be doubling down again on outsourcing, this time with tests that are being developed for teachers by the PARCC [http://www.fldoe.org/parcc] and SMARTER [http://www.k12.wa.us/SMARTER/default.aspx] multi-state consortia. We're not hearing much yet about how these systems will help teachers learn more about classroom assessment practices like the ones described in "Inside the Black Box."

One of the moves Finnish schools made in their concerted effort toward school improvement was to leverage local teacher-generated formative assessments, and they did so by investing deeply in professional development. Just one generation down the line, Finland has moved from a country with lackluster international achievement to one of the highest-achieving nations in the world.

We've said it before and will say it again: Teachers need what students need to grow and learn. They need vision, purpose, and focused assistance provided over time to meet the purpose (Tharp & Gallimore, 1988). And in addition, to quote Zavitovsky (2012) again,

Teachers and students both learn best when they can depend on frequent, high-quality feedback about the work they do. For the most part, the feedback we're getting from outsourced assessment systems is poorly designed to improve either student or adult learning and does not support the goals of the Common Core.

Contextualized formative assessment is what is needed—and professional development will be needed to help teachers do this kind of work in ways that are tied to the CCSS.

The CCSS help every child to hit high standards.

We admire the CCSS's goal of "ensur[ing] that all students are college and career ready in literacy no later than the end of high school." We agree that "shift[ing] content . . . toward higher levels of cognitive demand" (Porter, McMaken, Hwang, & Yang, 2011, p. 106) is a worthwhile goal. Wiggins (2013) explains why:

> For 30 years we have known that even the best state standards are tested too leniently. . . . NAEP [National Assessment of Educational Progress] results have for decades revealed that what counts as proficient in every state is really a minimum competency level of performance in the wider world. . . . NAEP test results have consistently shown that our students are poor at meaning-making and transfer of learning—something to be highlighted in the new tests. Alas, what many critics of Common Core forget is that it has been politically untenable for states to fail or warn a third to a half of their students—yet, this is in fact the reality of where students stand in terms of genuine readiness.

Wiggins's argument is corroborated by the fact that 40% of incoming college freshmen are required to take remedial classes once they enter college.

The CCSS has been adopted by 45 states, the District of Columbia, four territories, and the Department of Defense Education Activity.

Wow, how did that happen? What an opportunity.

What's to Worry About

Despite what we see as the opportunity the CCSS can provide, many critiques have been offered as well from very diverse political perspectives. Some from the political right see the CCSS as an attempt to violate states' sovereignty and nationalize education. Some from the political left see an interest in profit rather than education as driving the CCSS and worry about an increased emphasis on high-stakes testing.

Indeed, as Parker (2013) puts it, opposition to the CCSS has created strange political bedfellows. When the Tea Party, Diane Ravitch, and many progressive literacy educators all find themselves on the same side of an issue, we know something unusual is up. For us, the worry is not so much about states' rights or about process, though we do think the CCSS are one more example of a kind of top-down education reform with too little consultation from a broad range of teachers. In addition to many of the concerns outlined above, we worry about the following.

We worry about teacher autonomy and the eroding of decades of literacy research on best practices in the face of a centralized education reform.

Should a set of government-mandated standards really dictate to teachers the proportion of texts in their curricula? While we will discuss the issue of informational versus literary texts throughout this book, our point here is that, as Diane Ravitch (2013) points out, "There is no reason for national standards to tell teachers what percentage of their time should be devoted to literature or information. Both can develop the ability to think critically." We trust teachers to create an intertextual curriculum that serves their students' needs and interest.

We worry that the CCSS will negatively affect the students who most need our support in their literacy learning, including English language learners and students who are all already underperforming.

Our worry is grounded in our fear of an undue emphasis on test scores as a measure of this particular reform. As Newkirk (2013) puts it, "The Common Core State Standards are joined at the hip to standardized tests, not surprising because both the College Board and the ACT had

> While we agree that all of our students deserve to benefit from rigorous standards, we worry that they may create a new division between haves and have-nots, as all standardized tests seem to do.

such a big role in their creation" (p. 4). While we agree that all of our students deserve to benefit from rigorous standards, we worry that they may create a new division between haves and have-nots, as all standardized tests seem to do. If all of our students are to meet the Standards, all of our students are going to have to receive the most powerful instruction we can offer. As you'll see in this book, we do not believe that teachers who follow the instructional ideas promulgated by the authors of the CCSS will be providing that kind of powerful instruction.

To be honest, we also worry about the undue influence of a single individual on American education. Speaking of David Coleman, one of the authors of the CCSS and perhaps their most visible advocate, Ravitch (2013) bluntly says, "Is there not something unseemly about placing the fate and future of American education in the hands of one man?" Although our intent here is not to vilify David Coleman, both his new position as president of the College Board and his animated advocacy of what CCSS-friendly instruction would look like send chills down our pedagogical spines.

Why? It's well known that David Coleman has never been a teacher. But as you'll see throughout this book, what worries us even more is that his public pronouncements about how to teach to the Standards do not reflect an interest in or knowledge of educational research.

We think that these critiques of the CCSS are important to consider, but they do not affect the fact that 45 states have adopted them. What seems to us to matter most right now is working to ensure that their adoption results in more *effective* and *engaging* instruction for all students. That's why we need to think about not only what the CCSS require but also what they leave out, for those omissions may result in curricula and instruction that are neither effective nor engaging.

What the Standards Leave Out

In a nutshell, pleasure and wisdom. We believe that reading for pleasure is an important educational goal for all students. We believe that seeking wisdom is an equally important goal. Neither is articulated or appears to be valued within the CCSS document (NGA Center/CCSSO, 2010a).

Pleasure

As literacy teachers, we have long considered one of our primary roles as English teachers to be helping our students take pleasure not only in the texts we offer them in our classrooms but in the act of reading altogether. To capture this goal, Deborah often quotes Wordsworth with her preservice teachers: "What we have loved, others will love, and we will teach them how."

For us, reading is such a meaningful, powerful, and central part of our personal as well as professional lives that we want to make certain that our students can experience the same richness and pleasure we do. Isn't that one of the primary reasons why we became literacy teachers?

Of course, we agree with the authors of the CCSS that reading is a skill. All three of us write and talk with teachers about the skills required to read well (see, for example, Deborah's *Reading Better, Reading Smarter: Designing Literature Lessons for Adolescents* [Appleman & Graves, 2012] and Michael and Jeff's *Fresh Takes on Teaching Literary Elements: How to Teach What Really Matters About Character, Setting, Point of View, and Theme* [Smith & Wilhelm, 2010]). Yet we also believe that ELA instruction is about much more than teaching skills. It is this concern, that the CCSS fail to emphasize the pleasures of reading, that has English teachers all over the country filled with worry.

Where does this concern come from? In part, from the supplementary material to the CSSS document. Coleman and Pimentel (2012), for example, explain that materials aligned to the CCSS will include "a significant percentage of tasks and questions are text dependent"—that is, that "do not require information or evidence from outside the text or texts." Coleman (2011) was even more outspoken when talking about writing: "As you grow up in this world you realize people really don't give a [shit] about what you feel or what you think," a sentiment that would certainly seem to discourage "text-to-self" questions—questions such as "Has this ever happened to you? What were your feelings when you read this?" He makes a similar point in talking about teaching King's "Letter From Birmingham Jail":

> The first and most important is to let the mysteries that the
> letter provokes be the source of student motivation and your

interest rather than anything about you or anything I presume about you or your history. In other words, what we've done much too much is tried to go outside the text to motivate kids.

David Coleman is not alone in making this argument. David Liben, one of the contributing writers of the Common Core Appendix A explains, "It would be absurd to say you don't ever want to connect a text to kids' lives and experiences. But it should be *after* [emphasis added] you have mined from the text every insight and understanding you can" (quoted in Varlas, 2012).

Really? We don't think that students will be motivated to "mine every insight and understanding" if we don't encourage those text-to-self connections from the very start and help students see how the "Letter" matters in the here and now. And it is those very connections from which much of our pleasure about reading springs as is made very clear by the respondents in Jeff and Michael's (Wilhelm & Smith, 2014) study of the nature and variety of pleasure that adolescents take from their out-of-school reading. Here's testimony from one of them:

> Sometimes when, like, big stuff happens in my life, I'll think about what my favorite character would have done, the ones I admire most. Also, sort of subconscious. I don't stop and think about what someone would do, it's just something that happens. Like, I bet so-and-so would be really brave about this, or, one of my favorite characters would have totally sped after this guy. And then sometimes I follow their example and sometimes I don't. . . . They all have different approaches, different ways they approach things, and then I try to apply that to my life, to see which way works for me. Characters are just ways of thinking, really.

Isn't this kind of response just what we want as teachers?

David Pearson (as quoted in MacLennan, 2012) asserts that the Core expresses a fear of "constructivism run amuck" or of subjective forms of reader response that are merely associative and not respectful of the text and its construction, but this turning away from the affective domain ignores robust theories of transactional and authorial reader response that accommodate students' affect while at the same time paying careful attention to textual content and construction.

But as Claire Needell Hollander (2013), a middle school English teacher, argues in an op-ed piece for the *New York Times,* there need not be a conflict between the perceived emphasis on the reading skill and how English teachers emphasize the affective response in reading. She affirms the important role that emotions play as English teachers consider how to engage their students in reading. In contrast, she claims, the authors of the Standards pay little attention to emotion, resulting in what she calls a "bloodless effort."

For teachers of literature, emotion is not the enemy of reading skill; it is one of the *goals* of reading skills. And reading for pleasure or for personal meaning does not exist separately from the kinds of close reading the CCSS calls for; it exists alongside of it. Decades ago, Louise Rosenblatt (1938) reminded us that informational or efferent reading and aesthetic or pleasurable reading exist on a continuum and continually interplay within a reader. That is, Rosenblatt notes that during any one reading experience, readers may shift back and forth along a continuum between efferent and aesthetic modes of reading. Thus, in adopting an aesthetic stance, a reader may briefly focus on analyzing the formal properties of a text. Similarly, in an efferent stance, a reader may be stimulated to remember a related personal experience (Church, 1997). Rosenblatt reminds us that both kinds of readings are required: "Always, therefore, a full understanding of literature requires both a consciousness of the reader's own 'angle of refraction' and any information that can illuminate the assumptions implicit in the text" (1938, p. 115). In the context of her middle school English classroom, Hollander (2013) affirms this emphasis on both kinds of reading and laments that the CCSS focus on decontextualized skills and ignore the importance of emotion in the reading process.

We've heard our mentor George Hillocks many times say a version of the following: "Teaching is a transitive verb! It takes a direct and an indirect object. You teach something to somebody or you teach somebody something—to ignore the somebody means you are not teaching!" George's point is that we need to focus not only on what the reader is to able to do, but on who the reader is, his or her prior interests, motivation, need to know, and so on.

> We believe that reading for pleasure is an important educational goal for all students. We believe that seeking wisdom is an equally important goal.

Wisdom

When we think about our lives as readers, we realize just how important our reading has been for the way we've tried to live our lives. We want to be mindful that reading can have the same impact on our students. How we wish that the focus would be on "career, college, AND *citizenship* readiness." That said, it's on us as teachers to create classroom environments that honor diversity, that require students to work together in various configurations, that confront them with multiple perspectives on various issues, and that help students interrogate themselves and their own positions to develop new angles of vision. As Proust wrote, "The only true voyage would be not to visit strange lands but to possess other eyes." Possessing these other eyes, knowing how to work with people with other eyes, developing a reciprocal mind-set and a willingness to withhold judgment and look at all sides of an issue—all these are necessary for democratic citizenship in the 21st century.

We'd also like to see *an emphasis on higher purposes* for learning and for understanding. We'd like to see a focus on applying what is learned in the context of students' lived experience, in the disciplines, and out in the world. No kid was ever motivated to learn to read by the *cr*-blend or was motivated to read by a focus on inferencing. But we know from our own students that they will learn the very complex strategies featured in the Core *if* they have a reason to do so and a context of use that will reward their application.

When we read, we read to understand others: characters, authors, and by implication, people who are different from us in culture, experience, time, and space. This is essentially an ethical pursuit. When we compose for others, we compose—as the CCSS explicitly states—to create particular meanings and effects. In other words, we are working to convince other people to experience, believe, know, or do certain things—and this is an act that is immersed in ethical considerations.

If we read or compose texts as autonomous objects unconnected to our lives or the world, then we read them without engaging emotionally with characters or situations and without taking positions for or against authors, characters, or the presented visions. This seems highly problematic to us.

As we have stated already and will continue to assert throughout these pages, we are more worried about the *implementation* of the Standards than we are about either their intent or their core (forgive the pun) content. And that's where all of us who are teachers come in, together. We can make the best of the CCSS by remaining true to our philosophy, wisdom, and practices. We know what works in the classroom. We can make that work with the CCSS.

Yes, there is much that is missing and potentially counterproductive about the CCSS. But as we asserted above, despite these missing elements, it is up to us to fill the gaps—and we can fill in the gaps. There is nothing in the CCSS that would keep us from doing so. The only thing that would keep us from doing so is a lack of vision, creativity, imagination, and initiative. Let us have our best practices define the CCSS, not the other way around. In the following chapters, we'll offer some specific research-based and classroom-tested suggestions for how we can do just that.

Let us have our best practices define the CCSS, not the other way around.

2 Old Wine in Broken Bottles

The Common Core State Standards and "Zombie New Criticism"

We closed our last chapter by explaining our worry that the Common Core State Standards (CCSS), in their emphasis on skills, fail to take pleasure and wisdom into consideration, the very reasons reading skills are worth developing in the first place. That omission from the Standards document (National Governors Association Center for Best Practices/Council of Chief State School Officers [NGA Centers/CCSSO], 2010a), we think, is the result of an impoverished understanding of both the New Criticism, the theory upon which the CCSS seem to be grounded, and reader-response criticism, which emerged as a humane corrective to the excesses of the New Criticism. We think that those two misunderstandings have led to proponents' of the CCSS advocating a kind of instruction that will be both stultifying and ineffective, a kind of instruction very much at odds with what we know about best practice. That kind of instruction is most clearly exemplified by Coleman's model lesson for "Letter From Birmingham Jail" (*Middle School ELA Curriculum Video*, 2012; *Discussion*

of the Common Core, 2011). We'll be sharing our critique of that kind of instruction throughout this book as well as of that particular lesson in Chapter 7, but before we do so, we think it's worthwhile to explore in some depth the misunderstandings that have given rise to so much perplexing instructional advice.

In order to do so, we'd like to offer an example of the kind of instructional practice that all three of us have advocated for and observed in our work with teachers across the country. We expect that you'll be able to see similarities between your own teaching and the literature lesson described below. After we describe it, we'll explain why David Coleman finds this kind of sensible and solid teaching inconsistent with the pedagogy he prescribes to be in alignment with the CCSS.

A Lesson From the Classroom

In Ms. White's 10th-grade American Literature class, the students are about to begin a new unit on the Harlem Renaissance. For today's lesson, the students will read Langston Hughes's poem "Harlem" (Hughes, 1990).

Before Ms. White passes out the poem, she asks her students to take out the journals that they wrote last night about a dream they have for the future. In small groups, they share their entries and then consider two questions Ms. White has written on the board:

- What are some factors that might keep your dream from coming true?

- How would you feel if your dream failed?

Annica talks about moving to a different city; JoJo talks about having a house for his family; Jeremiah discusses going to college; Maggie talks about traveling to Africa; Sarah wants to be a hairdresser; Abdul wants peace in his homeland. The discussion continues for about 15 minutes. Then Ms. White writes on the board:

Langston Hughes

Harlem

Deferred

She asks students to tell her what they know about Langston Hughes. Jonny says that he was African American. Maria remembers reading "I Too Sing America." Danny pipes in with "Mother to Son." Then Ms. White asks the class what Harlem is. A place in New York, a neighborhood, a center of African American life, a slum, and so on.

Then Ms. White asks students to define the word "deferred." Becca asks if she can look it up on her phone. She reads, "to put off, to postpone." Ms. White continues, "What about the poem we read yesterday, Abdul Wahad's "Dream"? What do you remember about how the speaker of that poem felt? What was his perspective on the idea of dreams?

"OK," Ms. White says, "now let's turn to the poem we will consider for today. What's the title, oh, "Harlem," hmm. Let's read it. First to yourselves, and then I will ask a volunteer to read it aloud. As you read, please underline any words that strike you as being particularly important. You can use our anchor chart to remind you of the clues that help us determine importance. And put a question mark next to any words or lines that you don't understand."

Not a bad start to a lesson, right? Think of how different Ms. White's class would be from the one we imagined in the last chapter. In keeping with her training as a literature teacher and with our articulated best practices, Ms. White has begun with pre-reading activities to enhance her students' textual experiences in several ways:

- She activates prior interest and background knowledge that students will need to bring to bear to understand the text.

- She foreshadows some possible themes that may spring from the students' reading of the text.

- She creates a link of relevance between the text and her students' experiences by asking them to think about dreams.

- She has them do some of the pre-reading work outside of class (journaling about dreams) to use instructional time efficiently.

- She reminds students of the poet and his previous work.

- She locates the poem geographically and geopolitically.

- She preteaches vocabulary central to the poem and ask students to pay attention to how vocabulary choice is essential to the meaning of a text, to the establishment of tone, and to the effect of a text on its readers.

- She makes an intertextual link between something they read the day before and the poem they will be reading today.

While literature teachers may recognize these pre-reading moves that Ms. White makes as indicative of our best practice, the following objections about Ms. White's lesson would be raised if we took David Coleman's advice about textual instruction in the context of the CCSS:

> First, she asks students to consider something about themselves in preparation for reading the text. In contrast to Coleman's (2011) famous (or infamous) pronouncement that we quoted in the last chapter, she seems to give a s*** about what her students feel and think. It's good that she does so, for what kids feel and think about the literature we teach is something that we literacy teachers *do* care about deeply and that we use to promote their engagement and understanding.

> Next, Ms. White provides both pre-reading and scaffolding, teaching moves that Coleman has indicated are not necessary (*Discussion of the Common Core*, 2011). In fact, he specifically prescribes that we abolish pre-reading from our instruction of texts. (Much more on that in our next chapter.)

> Then, Ms. White asks questions that are not strictly text dependent. Her questions about the poet and the setting are designed to enhance the students' comprehension as they read the poem, as well as their capacity to situate the poem and use it as a tool to think with about dreams, race, history, poetry, and other larger issues.

As we'll see in greater detail next chapter, activating relevant schema has been demonstrated to improve comprehension. Coleman believes these questions distract from time better spent on a close reading of the text. In fact, Coleman implores that we "stop focusing instruction on reading strategies, rather than on the text itself" (*Discussion of the Common Core State Standards,* 2011). We find this particularly ironic, since we consider many of the anchor standards themselves to be meta-strategies—that is, ways of producing significant understandings through the interaction with texts, both informational and literary.

Ms. White's instruction to have students mark the text as they read and to use the anchor chart she and her students developed is precisely the kind of instruction that Coleman eschews. (We'll be expanding on that point in Chapter 4.) In other words, much of what we see as good teaching—pre-reading, connecting texts to student experiences, providing a context for reading, and offering during-reading strategies to improve student comprehension—is *not* supported by the authors of the Common Core. For example, in his prelude to his model lesson of "Letter From Birmingham Jail," Coleman, specifically, in his words, "attacks" three common ways of introducing the text, including providing background information, using pre-reading strategies, and offering instruction in what he calls a "generic" reading strategy (*Middle School ELA Curriculum Video*, 2012).

Ms. White continues her teaching by preparing students to make two kinds of intertextual links, one between the poem and the texts of their lives and another between the poem and another poem, a move that Coleman might see as violating the principle that students be given "essential opportunities . . . to spend the time and care required for close reading and to demonstrate in-depth comprehension of a specific source" (Coleman & Pimentel, 2012). (More on that in Chapter 5.)

You get the idea. We think Ms. White is engaging in good teaching practices, yet those kinds of practices are challenged and undermined by some of the suggestions that Coleman offers to teachers. Coleman's stance reveals a fundamental misunderstanding of New Criticism and its application, which not only misrepresents the theory itself but actually works against the successful implementation of the CCSS. In other words, Coleman is critiquing the successful pedagogical practice of Ms. White and her colleagues across the country on the grounds of a fundamental misunderstanding about how readers derive meaning from texts.

Where the Authors of the Standards Go Wrong About Connecting Texts With Lived Experience

The CCSS document (NGA Center/CCSSO, 2010a) does not articulate a theory of meaning or reading. In fact, rather than articulating the theoretical foundations of the Standards and the instruction he champions, David Coleman and his colleagues (Coleman, 2011; Coleman & Pimentel, 2012) suggest some dry and mechanistic ways of close reading. For us, this seems to be a kind of theoretical regression, rejecting what we know about how to engage students with texts and moving back into a strange version of New Criticism, what our friend and literary scholar Peter Rabinowitz calls "Zombie New Criticism" (Bancroft & Rabinowitz, 2013, p. 7). This version of New Criticism caricatures reader-centered theories and completely ignoring other critical theories that have so animated discussion of literature and literary teaching for the last several decades. What makes us call it "Zombie New Criticism"? A look at the history of the New Criticism is useful for understanding where Coleman and his colleagues get it wrong.

History of New Criticism

New Criticism emerged in the 1930s and 1940s as a response to literary readings that depended far too heavily on facts drawn from outside the texts in question. New Critical readings sought to explain connections between textual form and textual meaning, suggesting that the latter grew out of the former. Linguistic features such as sound devices were assumed to have meaning, and the formal elements of texts could be seen as signposts for reading, both when those texts exemplified a form with perfect consistency or bucked against it in purposeful violation.

The New Criticism acted as a corrective to prior trends. Before New Critical methods were established, literary study was primarily historical, consisting of lists of authors and titles. These factual accounts of literature would perhaps suffice in Thomas Gradgrind's (the infamous headmaster in Dickens's *Hard Times* who's interested only in facts)

Coleman critiques the successful pedagogical practice of English teachers on the grounds of a fundamental misunderstanding about how readers derive meaning from texts.

schoolroom, though one wonders if such knowledge is profitable. At the same time, literary criticism was largely impressionistic, yielding statements like "Shakespeare's tragedies are morally edifying" or "Shelley's sonnets warm the heart."

In fact, interpretation itself seemed secondary to facts outside the text, such as the author's biography or the social history out of which the literary text emerged—so much so that actually reading the texts was deemed unnecessary to the study of works of literature (Graff, 1989). Criticism as impression, meanwhile, unduly privileged literary scholars, making them arbiters of taste and morality while evading actual scholarly investigation.

The New Criticism, in contrast, defined a series of concerns that tend to focus the reader's production of meaning: irony, paradox, ambiguity, and tension. These characteristics of a text ask readers to assess possible meanings, and they require skills of recognition and explanation.

New Critics argued that readers of literature need preparation for creating literary interpretations, and the methodology behind the New Criticism is designed to ensure consistent goals and rigorous investigation. Its progenitors believed that the best way to arrive at a unified view of a text was to start from within and read the text outward. The largest purpose was to provide an interpretive framework that offered a coherent set of principles for reading that would lead to consistent and verifiable interpretations. While contemporary readers and teachers might disagree with this goal, the point to be taken here is that the New Criticism was far more than just careful reading, although it certainly entailed that. As Bancroft and Rabinowitz (2013, p. 7) explain, it was a "strong position grounded in theoretical claims about the nature of language, the nature of meaning, the nature of poetry." That position attempted to ensure a systematic examination of a literary text that would lead to meaningful results in interpretative practice. To be done well, it required that readers possess scaffolded knowledge, specific interpretive tools, and attention to reading strategies. In other words, The New Critics did not reflexively repudiate skills, or strategies that would help a reader construct an appropriate interpretation of a text. One way that Coleman and his colleagues go wrong, then, is that they don't take

Coleman and his colleagues don't take up the theoretical claims of the New Critics in any real way, in effect, sucking the life out of the theory.

up the theoretical claims of the New Critics in any real way, in effect, sucking the life out of the theory.

New Criticism in Practice

To see how a New Critical interpretation might emerge, let's consider possible interpretations of William Shakespeare's Sonnet 130, "My Mistress' Eyes Are Nothing Like the Sun."

> My mistress' eyes are nothing like the sun;
> Coral is far more red than her lips' red;
> If snow be white, why then her breasts are dun;
> If hairs be wires, black wires grow on her head.
> I have seen roses damasked, red and white,
> But no such roses see I in her cheeks;
> And in some perfumes is there more delight
> Than in the breath that from my mistress reeks.
> I love to hear her speak, yet well I know
> That music hath a far more pleasing sound;
> I grant I never saw a goddess go;
> My mistress when she walks treads on the ground.
> And yet, by heaven, I think my love as rare
> As any she belied with false compare.

First, a prospective reader needs to be able to identify and understand the formal features of the text. He or she needs to pay close attention to the structure of the sonnet, the rhythm and rhyme scheme, the quatrains and couplets, the ways the lines are formed together, how they sound when read aloud. Once those features are heeded, readers are also faced with the grammatical features of Early Modern English such as the subjunctive mood ("if snow be white" or "if hairs be wires"), which is rarely found in our contemporary language, and they need to understand that this construction marks situations that are conditional or contrary to fact. Those conditions play a significant role in the understanding of this poem. A New Critical reading of this sonnet also requires attention

© Roy Mehta/Iconica/Getty
Images

to unfamiliar vocabulary, like "damask'd," "dun," and "belied." Because this is a metrical poem, students need to understand syntactic inversions, as in line 6: "No such roses see I in her cheeks."

Even this quick outline of what readers need to know and do to engage in a New Critical reading of the sonnet makes clear another significant problem with Coleman's version of the New Criticism: his failure to recognize the knowledge, strategies, and skills that need to be in place before a reader can have a meaningful encounter with a text. Without preparation by way of pre-reading instruction, less experienced students of literature would have difficulty even decoding some of the lines. For example, despite the fact that the Standards document itself acknowledges the occasional need for scaffolding "when necessary" (Coleman & Pimentel, 2012), Coleman, in his lesson on "Letter From Birmingham Jail," remarks on the fact that it is fine to let students struggle as they first encounter a text (*Middle School ELA Curriculum Video*, 2012).

Even after a reader has decoded this poem, interpretation of the poem requires that readers recognize irony and paradox. Without this ability to recognize irony, as one of Deborah's students said, "This would be just about a guy dissing his girlfriend." Meanwhile, paradox reveals what most readers believe this poem tells us: First, it is quite possible to love someone who does not match contemporary standards of physical beauty, and second, it is not the female lover who is under attack here, but rather the abstract and perhaps unfair standards to which women are held.

As we'll see in forthcoming chapters, Coleman not only argues against pre-reading instruction, he argues against strategy instruction. But an illustration of how a teacher might encourage New Critical reading provides a glimpse at how wrongheaded his arguments are.

When setting up a lesson to teach Shakespeare's Sonnet 130 according to New Critical standards, teachers might begin with the following pre-reading tasks:

- Look through the poem and identify any words that are not familiar to you; look up these words in a dictionary.

- Underline or write down any lines that you are not able to understand and say what features of the line create difficulty for you. Working with two or three other students, try to say what the meaning of these lines might be.

- Read through the poem line by line and attempt to rewrite each line as it might read in present-day English.

Once these tasks are complete, students might then be guided to seek out some of the features that New Criticism suggests will lead to productive interpretation. The following questions might focus the reader's attention on the ways in which the text anticipates interpretation:

- Explain the poem's method for providing descriptions of the narrator's lover. What do you think the purpose of these descriptions is? Can you describe the *tension* that you find within the poem?

- Can you find *irony* in the poem? If so, where is the irony and how does it work? What would be the purpose of writing such a poem as an ironic piece?

- Do you find *paradox* in the poem? If so, how would you describe and explain this paradox? How might paradox point you toward a unifying interpretation of the poem?

Without conscious attention to method in reading, we have no way of predicting what readers will find in this poem. Perhaps they will think it heartwarming to discover that the narrator (if they even have such a term for naming the first-person speaker and distinguishing this voice from that of Shakespeare himself) loves a woman in spite of her homeliness. Maybe they will even wonder if this poem gives us hints about Shakespeare's alleged attraction to people of his own gender, and perhaps this attraction might provide a commentary on the debauchery of the Carolinian age in England. By contrast, though, a New Critical reading will provide material for an interesting set of questions:

- Does this sonnet really suggest that the lover is homely, or is it merely that she cannot live up to the impossible standards created by hyperbolic love poems? In other words, is this poem satirical?

- How does the tension between idealized womanhood and actual womanhood cause us to look for a reconciliation of opposing romantic descriptions?

- How does the narrator ensure that we recognize the poem's irony in order to avoid a misreading?

- How does paradox provide a mechanism for the narrator to make claims about the nature of physical beauty?

This set of questions is clearly guided by New Critical concerns. Whether we believe that these questions lead us to the heart of the matter is another issue. What we can be sure of, though, is that New Critical readings will lead to a somewhat consistent set of interpretive choices and conclusions. This school of criticism clearly leads us through a discrete set of concerns about the poem that could not be examined without prerequisite understandings.

Why We Worry About the Return to New Criticism

Tom Newkirk (2013) worries that the Standards promote "a sterile view of reading," one that is informed by the ghost of the New Criticism. We can trace the ghostly vestiges of the New Criticism in the CCSS in some of the following:

- Insisting on solely text-based questions

- Eschewing the important connections between reader and text (what I. A. Richards [2004] rudely deemed mnemonic irrelevances)

- Discouraging intertextual connections, not only between other texts but the texts of the students' prior experiences with reading as well (Coleman, 2011; *Middle School ELA Curriculum Video*, 2012)

As Newkirk (2013) remarks,

The central message in their [the authors of the CCSS] guidelines is that the focus should be on "the text itself"— echoing the injunctions of New Criticism during the early and mid-1900s. The text should be understood in "its own terms." While the personal connections and judgments of the readers may enter in later, they should do so only after students demonstrate "a clear understanding of what they read." So the model of reading seems to have two stages—first a close reading in which the reader withholds judgment or comparison with other texts, focusing solely on what is happening within "the four corners of the text." And only then are prior knowledge, personal association, and appraisal allowed in.

This seems to me an inhumane, even impossible, and certainly unwise prescription. (p. 3)

Perhaps, in a desperate desire to reduce literary understanding for the psychometricians, Coleman mistakenly anticipates that his version of New Criticism could provide a kind of precision to standardize the processes of literary study and to be able to measure it. For example, in his much-viewed sample lesson for "Letter From Birmingham Jail" (see *Middle School ELA Curriculum Video*, 2012), Coleman models how to read the letter paragraph by paragraph, without any scaffolding, to "examine" how the text progresses, to "force attention," to "reveal" evidence. Speaking of "measuring" literary response, the relationships between Coleman, the standard makers, and the test makers have been noted by Newkirk and others as a "'conflict of interest," at best.

One can't help but recall the scene in the film *Dead Poets Society* (Haft, Witt, Thomas, & Weir, 1989) when the teacher, Stephen Keating, has a student read aloud the introduction to their poetry textbook, which demonstrates how to calculate the merit of the poem through a kind of ridiculous calculus, using both a vertical (for "importance") and a horizontal (for perfection) axis. Keating finds this preposterous, and he instructs his pupils to rip the introduction out of their books. "This is a battle, a war," he exclaims, "and the casualties could be your hearts and souls." While this is not an endorsement of that romanticized and troubling portrait of teaching, many teachers believe that the heart and souls of their students may indeed be at stake—as well as their capacity to engage with and make meaning of their transactions with literature.

The Humane Corrective of Reader Response: Why a New Theory of Reading Was Needed by Secondary Teachers

Perhaps because Coleman does not take up the theoretical assumptions of the New Criticism in any serious way, he fails to recognize challenges to those assumptions. Decades ago, in response to the New Criticism when it was actually "new," Louise Rosenblatt (1938) located the meaning of a text not in the "autonomous" text itself, as Coleman et al. seem to be trying to do, but within the "transaction" between the reader and the text: "The reading of any work of literature is, of necessity, an individual and unique occurrence involving the mind and emotions of some particular reader and a particular text at a particular time under particular circumstances" (p. 132). The decontextualized New Critical view of literature as autonomous artifact is what brought many literature teachers to view reader response as a profound and humane corrective (Applebee, 1993; Beach, 1993).

Many English teachers had been schooled in the New Criticism favored by their English professors and had indeed found that the close readings that the New Criticism yielded were often a profitable way to construct interpretations. However, the treatment of text as a static aesthetic object to be studied and the refusal to consider outside sociocultural forces as well as variations between readers did not work as well in the average middle or secondary classroom as it had in the college classroom. Adolescent readers, in the throes of identity development, seemed to yearn for ways to connect what they read in school with their lives outside of school. In fact, personal engagement with literary texts and connections between literature and personal experience proved to be an important way into texts for adolescent readers.

Fueled by the progressive movement and the Dewey-influenced Louise Rosenblatt, teachers came to believe that it was more important to encourage students to learn to construct their own meaning rather than divine a predetermined meaning in a kind of academic guessing game. Believing that literature was not simply an aesthetic object to be understood but both a mirror into our own experiences and a window into the experiences of others, progressive teachers tended to move away from the New Criticism.

Lois Tyson (2006) reminds us that "the New Critics believed that the timeless meaning of the text—what the text is—is contained in the text alone" (p. 170). Reader-response critics contend that "what a text is cannot be separated from what it does" (p. 170). The role of the reader, then, and how he or she responds to any particular text, cannot be separated from our understanding of the text itself. Readers are not passive recipients of a stable, fixed, meaning; rather, they create dynamic meanings as they read. It is not surprising that secondary teachers found the importance that reader response placed on readers a more friendly and inviting theory in which to situate their literature teaching than was New Criticism.

As Deborah has written elsewhere,

> This new focus on the reader indisputably enlivened and irrevocably altered the teaching of literature. It changed or supposedly changed the power dynamics in the classroom and the role of the teacher, and it clearly changed what it was that we asked students to do when they read texts. The paradigmatic shift from a text-centered to a reader-centered pedagogy also changed our consideration of the kinds of texts we used. We found ourselves sometimes considering whether a particular text was teachable by the degree to which it might invoke personal responses from our students. From the point of view of most observers, at least, these were all changes for the better. (Appleman, 2009, pp. 29–30)

The Admitted Excesses of Reader Response

Yet in some ways, as a profession, we overcorrected. In some cases we threw the text out with the bathwater, leaving some pretty sloppy practices that encourage personal revelation at the expense of textual interpretation. In *Reshaping High School English,* in a chapter tellingly titled "Beyond Barney and the Cult of the Individual," Pirie (1997) reflects on the practice of valorizing individual responses in the literature classroom and the inherent dangers and complications of that approach. As English teachers, we may have been guilty of overprivileging and romanticizing the individual at the expense of considerations of context and text. Pirie warns, "We now need to question the limits of the doctrine of individualism before our classroom practices harden into self-perpetuating rituals" (p. 9). This is, in part, what James Marshall (1991) meant when he called reader response our new orthodoxy. Pirie (1997) also questions whether a personal response approach to literature is justifiable from the perspective of academic rigor: "I am, however, suspicious of the suggestion that just expressing your personal response is a satisfactory educational attainment, or that such a response could be evaluated for its authenticity" (p. 12). Of course, Rosenblatt herself never intended these excesses; her transactional theory of response squarely situates the text itself as an equal factor in the construction of meaning.

In their book *Authorizing Readers*, Peter Rabinowitz and Michael Smith (1998) echo this sentiment when they argue that it's "important for readers and teacher to have a theoretical model that allows them to critique readings" (p. 121). Meaning is a result of a kind of negotiation between recognizing the clues for how an author envisioned a text being read that are embedded in the construction of the text itself and the reader's response. It is not simply the question "What does this mean to me?" that Smith says captures the essence of reader-centered theories. How can literature foster knowledge of others when we focus so relentlessly on ourselves and our own experiences?

This focus on factors that exist outside the text, including personal experiences, some observers feel, left little time for the text itself and for the explicit teaching of increasingly complex texts. And we do confess that reader response sometimes lost its way in some secondary classrooms, losing the text and becoming a kind of autobiographic springboard of too much information, or as our students might say, *TMI*. It is these kinds of instructional excesses to which Coleman objects (Coleman, 2011; *Middle School ELA Curriculum Video*, 2012). Yet what he objects to is not found either in the response theories that inspire our practices or in those practices themselves.

So on the one hand, we worry that the adoption of the CCSS, especially the adoption of what we view as David Coleman's impoverished vision of literary instruction, will bring the tenants of New Criticism, for better and for worse, more fully into the secondary classroom. And on the other hand, we recognize some of the excesses that stemmed from valo-rizing readers at the expense of the texts. Perhaps we can come up with some kind of hybrid version. Our point here is not to plea for literary instruction to return to the excesses of "extreme" reader response but, rather, to a place between that caricature and the zombie version of the New Criticism that Coleman animates.

How You Can Get It Right

A Compromise Approach: Teaching in Alignment With the CCSS and Our Own Best Practices

At the beginning of this chapter, we presented Ms. White's approach to teaching Langston Hughes' poem "Harlem." We presented the lesson as an example of good solid pedagogical practice. And it is. We also discussed particular elements of the lesson that give rise to the kinds of unfounded criticism offered by David Coleman and the other coau-thors of the CCSS. While we stand by that first lesson as illustrative of a kind of good practice, we want to offer another example of a literature lesson, one that much more *intentionally* incorporates the intent of the CCSS. Through this sample lesson, we hope to be able to combine our best practices—including the kinds of pre-reading, frontloading, and personal engagement approaches to which Coleman objects—with the kinds of close reading, formalist, and text-dependent questions that are advocated by the authors of the CCSS.

We've chosen to teach Li-Young Lee's (1986) "The Gift," a poem that we think is appropriate for 9th through 12th graders, to provide an exam-ple. It is not an easy poem to understand, yet it uses simple, everyday language. We think it satisfies both demands for text complexity and accessibility. This is another place where we think the authors of the CCSS get it wrong. Their definition of text complexity, as we further explore in Chapter 6, is simplistic and misleading. This poem is a case in point, demonstrating multiple layers of text complexity, often disguised by deceptively simple vocabulary.

Pre-Reading Activities

As we discussed above, contrary to Coleman's extreme version of New Criticism, there is no reason why some modest pre-reading activities couldn't be used to great effect to prepare students for engagement and success with the reading. In keeping with some New Critical practice, we might focus on the title and ask students to predict what kind of gift might be involved. We might give some biographical information about Li-Young Lee, if we thought it would enhance students' reading of the poem. We find, for example, that students appreciate knowing that they are reading a contemporary work by a living poet. We also might pre-teach the word "assassin," as it is used in an unusual way and might trip up students as they read.

In addition to these text-specific activities, we'd also ask students to do some autobiographical writing before they read the poem. For example, we might ask students to write about a little event that had a big impact on them. We might also ask them to list some of the best gifts they have ever received and consider them in terms of the giver, the context in which the gift was given, the significance of the gift, and whether it was a material gift.

Questions for Discussion

In the best New Critical tradition, here are some text-dependent questions that will deepen students' reading of the poem:

- Who is the speaker in the poem? Why is it important to notice who is speaking in the poem?"

- Who is the audience of the poem?

- What is the situation and setting of the poem?

- Describe the structural pattern of the poem both in terms of visual patterns and sound patterns (stanzas, rhyme scheme, meter, free verse, alliteration, repetition, etc.). How do these patterns contribute to your overall sense of what the poem is trying to do?

- List some interesting uses of words or diction that you noticed. Next to each "noticing" write down what that choice made you think of.

- What does the speaker mean when he calls his father's voice a prayer?

- What story does the poem tell? Would you call this a narrative poem?

- Comment on figurative language (metaphor, extended metaphor, simile, idiom, personification).

- We've been noticing the ways that authors signal that something is symbolic—for example, what seems like undue attention to a minor detail and so on. Did you notice any symbols here? What did the author do to signal it/them?

- Is the poem allegorical?

- How does the title relate to the poem?

- How does the speaker feel about "the gift"? What lines support your conclusion?

(Some of these questions were adapted from a lesson found at http://katieseng1.edublogs.org/2010/03/31/the-gift-analysis-advanced-placement-format.)

We'd also suggest asking some questions that ask students to focus on their experience of reading, a kind of question that Coleman would critique as leading students away from the text:

- What images came to mind as you read the poem? Which images lingered? What kinds of feelings did those images evoke?

- What words would you use to describe your feelings toward the poem?

- How old do you think the speaker is?

- Did the poem bring any similar experiences to mind?

- How is this poem like or unlike other poems we've read together?

Follow-Up Activities

A variety of activities would be excellent follow-ups to the discussion:

- Students might be asked, individually or in small groups, to offer an oral reading of the poem and explain the choices they made in performing it.

- We might also ask students to evaluate the advice Li-young Lee gives in the poem. Is it good advice, to parents, to friends?

- After their reading, students could view Li-Young Lee reading the poem: http://billmoyers.com/content/pure-poetry

- Students might be asked to write their own poem or story, titled "The Gift," describing a real-life situation that has some resonance with the one described in the poem. (Sorry, David—we think these literature–life connections *are* valuable.)

This lesson does not discard decades of best practice. And in adhering to what we know, it addresses the following CCSS:

CCSS.ELA-Literacy.RL.9-10.2. Determine a theme or central idea of a text and analyze in detail its development over the course of the text, including how it emerges and is shaped and refined by specific details; provide an objective summary of the text.

CCSS.ELA-Literacy.RL.11-12.4. Determine the meaning of words and phrases as they are used in the text, including figurative and connotative meanings; analyze the impact of specific word choices on meaning and tone, including words with multiple meanings or language that is particularly fresh, engaging, or beautiful. (Include Shakespeare as well as other authors.)

CCSS.ELA-Literacy.RL.11-12.6. Analyze a case in which grasping a point of view requires distinguishing what is directly stated in a text from what is really meant (e.g., satire, sarcasm, irony, or understatement).

CCSS.ELA-Literacy.RL.11-12.7. Analyze multiple interpretations of a story, drama, or poem (e.g., recorded or live production of a play or recorded novel or poetry), evaluating how each version interprets the source text. (Include at least one play by Shakespeare and one play by an American dramatist.)

CCSS.ELA-Literacy.RL.11-12.10. By the end of grade 11, read and comprehend literature, including stories, dramas, and poems, in the grades 11–CCR [college and career readiness] text complexity band proficiently, with scaffolding as needed at the high end of the range.

By the end of grade 12, read and comprehend literature, including stories, dramas, and poems, at the high end of the grades 11–CCR text complexity band independently and proficiently.

This lesson demonstrates that we *can* come to some kind of pedagogical compromise. We can help our students meet the CCSS, without losing the kinds of active engagement strategies that have proved effective and essential in literature instruction. We will present an even more elaborated example in our final chapter, presenting our alternative to Coleman's now infamous lesson on "Letter From Birmingham Jail."

Sticking With the Standards (Not With the Instructional Mandates That Showed Up Later)

David Coleman's version of New Criticism isn't even fair to the New Critics. Even more importantly, his version of teaching texts (Coleman, 2011; *Discussion of the Common Core*, 2011; *Middle School ELA Curriculum Video*, 2012) can wreak havoc on our hard-earned, considered, and deliberative pedagogies. As Alan Sitomer asks (2012), should we really be learning how to cook from someone who's never been in the kitchen, especially when the fare is literature? Sitomer's point is particularly salient as we consider Coleman's admonishments against the kinds of teaching strategies that have proved so effective over the last few decades. Why is Coleman so easily able to dismiss these strategies? Because he's never had to use them. His literary experience as an Ivy League academic coupled with his lack of classroom teaching experience with secondary students make it easy to understand why his preferred methodology of choice would echo many of the tenants of the New Criticism. A Yale-educated Rhodes scholar who studied English literature at Oxford and classical educational philosophy at Cambridge, Coleman actually publically joked about his lack of qualifications for shaping the Standards (Thomas, 2013). In Coleman's world of literary experience, the text is the thing and there is no need for the often-unpredictable yet

How can we help our students become skilled readers if we don't give students the opportunity to find their way between the literary (and informational) texts and contexts in which they live, both in and out of the classroom?

amazingly rich realities of classroom life to intrude. In Alan Sitomer's world, the world of a career, award-winning secondary teacher, the students before him and their dispositions, prior knowledge, and skills are essential to the decisions that he makes to help construct successful literary experiences. It is no wonder that their conceptions of what constitutes sound pedagogical practice in the teaching of text differ so dramatically. And we're investing in the advice and opinion of Alan the teacher, not David, the academician. We shudder, however, to think whose view of literary teaching will prevail.

We like Robert Scholes's (2001) notion of the "crafty reader." Scholes believes interpreting literature can be learned and practiced and demystified but that the act of reading and interpretation cannot be separated from the lived experiences of readers:

> We must open the way between the literary and the verbal
> text and the social text in which we live. (p. 24)

Not one of the Standards, not one, asks students to consider the relationship between the text and lived experience, whether it's the reader's or the broader context in which we live, learn, and read. How can we help our students become skilled and crafty readers if we don't bring the outside in, if in our literature classrooms we don't give students the opportunity to find their way between the literary (and informational) texts and social contexts in which they live, both in and out of the classroom?

It is important to note that while the Core does not specifically address these important considerations, the anchor standards themselves in no way forbid or preclude them. In fact, the CCSS document clearly states the following: "Teachers are thus free to provide students with whatever tools and knowledge their professional judgment and experience identify as most helpful for meeting the goals set out in the Standards" (NGA Center/CCSSO, 2010a, p. 4). If we adhere to the Standards document itself (and not to Coleman's comments about it) then it comes down to us to determine how to retain these essential elements of our teaching—for the benefit of our students, ourselves, and our profession.

Using the Most Powerful Resource We Have for Teaching Students Something New

3

The Case for Background Knowledge

In our introduction, we explained that we support the Common Core State Standards (CCSS; albeit with different levels of enthusiasm), though we have some worries. One of the things we like most about the CCSS is their explicit recognition that instructional decisions are best left in the hands of teachers. As the CCSS document puts it in its discussion of key design considerations, "The Standards define what all students are expected to know and be able to do, not how teachers should teach" (National Governors Association Center for Best Practices/ Council of Chief State School Officers, 2010a).

Where the Authors of the Standards Go Wrong About Pre-Reading Instruction

That is how it should be. Teachers are professionals and ought to be given professional decision-making

power. Teachers ought to be the ones to determine how they will best meet standards in their own classrooms with their own highly unique set of specific human beings sitting in the desks in their particular classroom in the specific culture of their own school and community. There is no other expert than the classroom teacher on how to teach his or her own specific students in the context of their own lives and social situations. That's why it's so disconcerting to hear what David Coleman, one of the chief authors and leading proponents of the CCSS, has been saying about the kind of teaching that will help achieve them. In this chapter, we'll elaborate on a concern we introduced in Chapter 2: Coleman's exhortation to dispense with pre-reading instruction.

Coleman has been very explicit about his disdain for pre-reading activities. When he explains how he would teach Martin Luther King's "Letter From Birmingham Jail" (Coleman, 2011) he starts by "attacking" (his word) the three most common ways teachers typically begin their instruction:

- *Providing background information* (his examples: King was a great leader . . . He wrote the letter because . . .)

- *Assigning pre-reading activities* (his example: having students predict what might be in the letter)

- *Announcing a mini-lesson on a skill* (e.g., today, we're going to do main idea, and you'll read the letter looking for the main idea)

Here's how his attitude toward pre-reading activities was characterized by one commentator (Porter-Magee, 2012):

> Coleman is refreshingly unapologetic in his assertion that pre-reading activities are a waste of instructional time. He believes, for instance, that giving students background information about the text does little more than encourage students to parrot back the teacher's words when answering questions, rather than actually absorbing and critically analyzing what the author said. And he thinks spending time predicting what the text is going to be about or comparing it to other works is a needless distraction. Instead, he encourages teachers to allow students to dive immediately in to the text itself.

Why It Matters

Let's begin by noting that how teachers introduce texts in their classrooms is an empirical question and Coleman provides no empirical support for his assertion that teachers do it in the way he describes. But that's just the start of the problems.

More significantly, what he describes as pre-reading is not at all what we see expert teachers doing, nor is it what we have for many years been promoting in our own work (see Appleman, 2010; Smith & Wilhelm, 2010). His is an impoverished and gross misrepresentation and underrepresentation of good teaching. It makes us wonder what Coleman knows about teaching in the first place. For instance, pre-reading, or as we call it, frontloading, is far different from what he describes and always extends far beyond providing fact-based background knowledge helpful to comprehension, as important as that is. Nor are pre-reading activities solely about making predictions. They are about activating students' prior interests and background knowledge—both conceptual and procedural/strategic—so that these prior understandings are available as resources for the new challenges provided by a complex text.

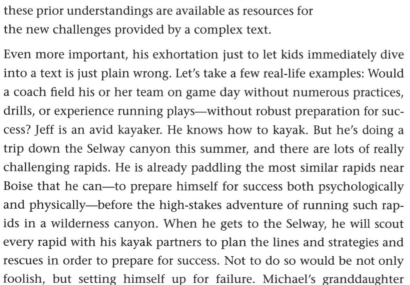

Even more important, his exhortation just to let kids immediately dive into a text is just plain wrong. Let's take a few real-life examples: Would a coach field his or her team on game day without numerous practices, drills, or experience running plays—without robust preparation for success? Jeff is an avid kayaker. He knows how to kayak. But he's doing a trip down the Selway canyon this summer, and there are lots of really challenging rapids. He is already paddling the most similar rapids near Boise that he can—to prepare himself for success both psychologically and physically—before the high-stakes adventure of running such rapids in a wilderness canyon. When he gets to the Selway, he will scout every rapid with his kayak partners to plan the lines and strategies and rescues in order to prepare for success. Not to do so would be not only foolish, but setting himself up for failure. Michael's granddaughter

Gabrielle loves to play games. Now board games all have some kind of "family" (Wittgenstein, 1953/2001, p. 27) resemblance, but whenever Michael plays a new game with her, he makes sure that she understands how this game compares to other games they have played in the past, and they rehearse the specific new rules and purposes of the particular game they'll be playing. Deborah prepares her student teachers by having them visit the classroom in which they'll be teaching several times in the months before they actually arrive on the first day of school in the fall. She asks them to familiarize themselves with the sounds, the smells, and the feel of the classroom and to spend the summer imagining themselves in that classroom so that they will feel more comfortable when their teaching actually begins. All of these stories have one thing in common—when we have the opportunity to plan and prepare, we are more successful, whether it's kayaking, playing a board game, or student teaching.

What we've learned from our life experience is borne out by the last 50 years of reading research. Here's how Allington and Cunningham (2010) begin a posting on education.com:

> The most important factor in determining how much readers will comprehend and how well writers will be able to communicate about a given topic is their level of knowledge about that topic (interest in the topic is also important but often is related to prior knowledge). The importance of prior knowledge to comprehension and communication is included in virtually all modern theories of reading (Anderson & Pearson, 1984; Pressley, Wood, & Woloshyn, 1992; Spivey, 1996).

As we'll see in greater detail later, the knowledge readers need has to be in place before they begin a text.

But it's not just reading research. Literary theorist Peter Rabinowitz (1987) titles his examination of literary reading *Before Reading* and explains in his introduction that "readers need to stand somewhere before they pick up a book, and the nature of that 'somewhere,' I argue, significantly influences the ways in which they interpret (and consequently evaluate) texts" (p. 2).

From the beginning of his career, George Hillocks, one of our personal mentors and a giant of literacy education research, has argued that the most powerful resources teachers have to teach students something new is what they already care and know about (Hillocks, McCabe, & McCampbell, 1971). In other words, if teachers do not make use of these resources, there's no way to assist a student to outgrow his or her current self since the current self has not been recognized and recruited for learning. The more a student struggles, is marginalized by mainstream culture, or possesses a damaged learner identity, the more important such activation and preparation for success will be.

The use of background knowledge is obviously necessary for inferencing (a major thrust of the CCSS, explicitly cited in reading Anchor Standard for 1, and implicated in reading Anchor Standards 2–6), as well as for analysis (explicitly cited in RS 2, 3, 5, and 9 and implicated in RS 2–9); you need background knowledge to make connections between things or fill in missing gaps. You also need it for both seeing connections throughout data and across data sets, and for applying new strategies independently (the ultimate goal of the CCSS).

> The more a student struggles, is marginalized by mainstream culture, or possesses a damaged learner identity, the more important such activation and preparation for success will be.

Our own research over the last 20 years has been organized around helping teachers help students meet new and ever more complex literacy challenges, and we've focused in particular on struggling and resistant learners. One of the central lessons of our careers is this: The most important time to teach is *before* students undertake a new challenge. We must therefore prepare students for success; we must be proactive versus reactive in responding to student needs.

Vygotsky's (1978) famous formulation has it that we all have a zone of actual development, a cognitive zone of accomplishment composed of what we already can do independently and without assistance. Vygotsky argued that learning occurs in the zone of *proximal* development, the zone where students can do something *with help* that they cannot yet do alone. The help they get to prepare them and assist them through the task that they cannot yet do alone is what Vygotsky would call *teaching*. If we go right to the challenging task, as Coleman wants, we have lost our best opportunity to teach.

We know that you've been told a joke you didn't get. You did one of two things: (1) You either laughed anyway to gloss over your lack of

One of the central lessons of our careers is this: The most important time to teach is *before* students undertake a new challenge.

understanding (something students do all the time in school), or (2) you asked a friend to explain the joke to you. Once it was explained, you didn't laugh. You might have said, "OHHH," or ironically intoned, "HA HA HA." Why? Because you can't rehabilitate a joke—if you don't get it on the first telling, then it can't be saved. The joy of a joke is knowing enough to "get it" on its first telling.

The same is true for a writing assignment or reading assignment. Once students begin to struggle and enter into what Jeff calls their ZFD (zone of frustrational development), the jig is up. The unique power of any aesthetic text, whether fictional or nonfictional, is that it doesn't directly tell what it means. Its power resides in the fact that you have to figure out the meaning. If a teacher tells a student what it means, then the student has lost the joy of figuring it out, and the text has lost its power to move, inform, and transform. This is why we need to prepare students for success, to build their conceptual and strategic toolbox and give them practice so that they can eventually independently succeed on the challenging tasks we provide them, tasks that the CCSS requires and that the world will require as well.

Recent research in neuroplasticity demonstrates the importance of modeling strategic use, then mentoring, providing for independent use, and monitoring of the application of new strategies. "Mirror neuron circuitry" (Damasio, 2005; Lakoff, 2008) is activated when we see a process modeled for us, allowing us to rehearse and lay down the neural pathways that help us to attempt the process for ourselves. This circuitry is activated even more strongly and then consolidated when we enact the process for ourselves (Lakoff, 2008, p. 117) and continue to practice it over time. Neuroscience has clearly shown that without such preparation we can become quickly frustrated and stymied by complex tasks and texts (Doidge, 2007).

Moreover, learning takes time and practice. Think of anything you've ever learned of any significance—from kissing to cooking—and you'll realize that you didn't get it right the first time. Someone was likely there to mentor you, someone who said, "Let's try that again," providing a little bit of assistance and guidance. That's how people learn—by practicing and approximating expertise ever more closely over time in a context of real use and by practicing with expert help.

The Anders Ericsson research (e.g., Ericsson & Lehman, 1996), made famous by Malcolm Gladwell (2008), established that 10,000 hours of focused, deliberate practice is necessary to gain expertise, based partly on Ericsson's finding that practice animates neurons and builds neural pathways through the brain, thus building ever-evolving new capacities. He also found that 3,000 hours of focused and assisted practice, practice that explicitly pushes one's capacities in the direction of expertise, is necessary to gain competence in any complex repertoire of skills, like those required for reading and writing. Are our students getting 3,000 hours of practice in reading and writing during their schooling? We don't think so. Practice before performance, as any coach knows, is the most effective way of providing that important assistance toward expertise.

To summarize Ericsson: Talent is the result of acquired skill. Skill acquisition requires taking a long and incremental view, engaging in constant practice geared toward real-world expertise, reflecting, and exhibiting the willingness to take risks and innovate. Think of the lessons of this research for us and for our students. Think of the promise of the CCSS if teachers K–12 work on the same few generative anchor standards for reading and composing argumentative, informational, and narrative text throughout the 12 years of a student's schooling, putting their own teacherly insights and innovations to play in service of this project.

Preparing Students to Comprehend

Since pre-reading is under attack, let's look at it in concrete terms. Here is a picture with which you might be familiar.

What image do you perceive first? Can you then perceive another image? We've done this activity with students of a variety of ages for going on 30 years. Most of them typically see the old woman first, who they often call a "witch," "hag," or "grandma." After all, most everyone is older than the students are, and so that picture is close to home for them and uses an available conceptual schema or organized set of knowledge about the world that is readily available to them.

Here's another thing: The old woman is in profile, so she fits students' schematic expectation regarding that you should see the subject's face in a portrait. Most students cannot see the younger woman, who is turned away, since this violates their genre expectation for a portrait. But show them a photograph of a "Gibson Girl" from the 1890s, and they can instantly see the second picture. Why? They can use the photograph as a conceptual frontload that allows them to see the young woman in the engraving. The photo is a resource that provides the background knowledge necessary to success in perceiving something new and outside their prior experience. It is impossible to perceive what you don't already know something about.

Here's a textual example that illustrates the crucial importance of prior knowledge. Imagine that you encounter the following little sentence "Blinds for sale" and have to answer two questions: How much can you expect to pay, and what will you need to transport your purchase? Generally, when most people read this statement, they activate background knowledge about window treatments and venetian blinds to make sense of the text. But now imagine if the statement continues this way: "Goose hunting season opens soon." The answers to both questions change substantially. Many students have difficulty making the kind of switch we just asked you to make. But if they activated the correct schema beforehand, they would have a greater chance of being successful.

Here's another example. Imagine seeing the sentence "She ran quickly toward the rising sun." Not only do expert readers activate a schema as soon as they start to read and monitor the appropriateness and change the schema as needed, they also use the schema to visualize what is going on. Most of the students we've used this activity with profess to see an athlete taking her morning run or maybe a young woman running down the beach toward her lover. But imagine that the statement continues with this: "knowing fresh oats would be in the barn." Sometimes students will stick with their original schema and say something like "they must be serving oatmeal in the barn."

(One student from a rural school once said: "Oh, it must be a cow!" and all the farm kids laughed at her. Why? Cows don't eat oats; they eat grasses. That is how important background knowledge is to comprehension.)

There is a cognitive bias toward sticking with one's original schema (known variously as confabulation, mental intrusion, or affective/cognitive priming;

see Haidt, 2006). One of the most significant signposts of expert reading is the ability to monitor for schema appropriateness and recruit new schema as necessary (Anderson & Pearson, 1984). Students who understand that they bring conceptual schema to bear when they read would also have a much better chance of monitoring and self-correcting when they are in the wrong schema.

Here's a more extended textual example:

> With hocked gems financing him
> Our hero defied all scornful laughter
> That tried to prevent his scheme
> Your eyes deceive
> He had said
> An egg
> Not a table
> Typifies this unexplored planet
> Now three sturdy sisters sought proof
> Forging along sometimes through calm vastness
> Yet more often over turbulent peaks and valleys
> Days become weeks
> As many doubters spread fearful rumors
> About
> The Edge
> At last from somewhere
> Welcome winged creatures appeared
> Signifying momentous success (Dooling & Lachman, 1971, p. 217)

Our students almost always fail to identify the topic and the meaning of this poem. They comprehend all the words, but they cannot access the schematic background necessary to transacting and making meaning with this text. One student explained how the poem was about the rock band U2, whose guitarist is named "The Edge." That student took the only thing he recognized and built an interpretation from that, confabulating like crazy all the way, which is what all of us have a cognitive bias to do. He had to confabulate because he had not activated the necessary resources to making a reasonable interpretation with the details of the text.

Now imagine frontloading the reading by chanting: "In 1492 . . ." The chant immediately brings to mind what students know about Columbus. A chorus of "Ahhhs" can be heard as they activate their background knowledge; share that knowledge to help students, like ELLs who may not know about Columbus; and then apply it to the text, making everything click into place. The hocked gems are Queen Isabella's jewels; the three sturdy sisters are the *Nina*, the *Pinta*, and the *Santa Maria*; and so on.

We have found in our own classroom research with struggling readers that the majority of reading comprehension problems can be solved by simply activating background interests and knowledge that students already possess (see Wilhelm, Baker, & Dube, 2001). If students do not know enough—whether conceptually, procedurally, or generically (i.e., about the text type)—then the best time to build this knowledge is before they read a text that places such demands on them.

Here's another example, from the seminal schema research by Bransford and Johnson (1972):

> A newspaper is better than a magazine. A seashore is a better
> place than the street. At first it is better to run than to walk.
> You may have to try several times. It takes some skill but
> is easy to learn. Even young children can enjoy it. Once
> successful, complications are minimal. Birds seldom get in the
> way. Rain, however, soaks in very fast. Too many people can
> cause problems. It can be very peaceful. A rock will serve as
> an anchor. If things break loose, however, you will not get a
> second chance. (p. 722)

Most of our students again cannot make meaning of this text. Again, there are no vocabulary problems. The issue is one of schema activation. But once someone indicates that the passage must be about a kite, everything clicks into place. In this example, the obvious schema markers were deleted and replaced with neutral words. And this example is actually what a textbook excerpt looks like to a student who has no background knowledge of the topic. You cannot comprehend when you have no background knowledge to bring to bear. This is why frontloading is not only important to reading, but also necessary to it.

Expert readers know how to activate essential background prior to reading and how to get background information that they lack. Students may not have that knowledge, or if they do, they may not activate it. As a consequence, if teachers want students to understand and enjoy the reading they do in class, they have to help students develop the knowledge they need *before* they begin reading. And if teachers want students to be able to understand and enjoy the reading they do outside school, teachers have to help them develop the strategies expert readers employ in their own reading so that they become independently able to do this.

In short, the takeaway is this: *The most important time to teach is before reading—or writing—or learning anything new.*

Good frontloading changes and expands the zone of proximal development and pushes the zone of frustrational development farther away. Frontloading *is* teaching, and it is the most powerful kind of teaching: instructional assistance that is proactive and prepares students for success.

How You Can Get It Right: Five Strategies That Connect Students With Critical Concepts

We hope that we've convinced you that Coleman's statements about frontloading are wrong. Pre-reading instruction is necessary if students are to have meaningful transactions with texts. So what to do? We have five suggestions.

1. Apply Background Knowledge

First, we suggest using the pictorial and textual examples we've presented to convince students that they have to apply what they already know when they read. We've found that they may be reluctant to do so. One striking example comes from Jeff's *You Gotta BE the Book* (Wilhelm, 2008):

> Marvin read aloud that "Jack slid into second and kuh-nocked his kuh-nee," pronouncing both silent k's. When asked what a "kuh-nee" could possibly be, Marvin shrugged.

"I just told you what it says. How should I know what it means?" Marvin often indicated that it was the reader's job to pronounce words, but not to make meaning.

When asked if he could "see" what was happening in the story, Marvin replied, "No." Marvin offered that he had both played baseball and been a spectator at baseball games. So he was asked what body parts one was likely to injure when sliding into second base. Eventually, Marvin acknowledged that the "kuh-nee" was probably a "knee."

Later in the story I asked Marvin who was behind the plate calling balls and strikes.

"It doesn't say," he informed me, which was true in the literal sense.

"But Marvin," I asked, "you play baseball. Who calls balls and strikes?"

"The umpire," he replied. "But it doesn't say who's doing it here!" When I pursued the issue, he pushed the story across the desk to me and said, "Okay, you find it. Go ahead. You find it then!" (p. 129)

Students who have been conditioned to look for the right answer in the text are sometimes reluctant to make even the most obvious of inferences. We may have to teach them that authors count on their applying background knowledge when they read.

2. Use Visual Texts

Visual texts provide powerful opportunities to frontload future reading, especially for striving and ELL readers. There are several ways to use visuals to frontload:

Floorstorming

Students are provided with photographs or pictures of events, ideas, people, and the like that are related to the unit topic or essential question.

Students spread the images out on the floor and group or classify them in different ways, all the while working to infer the topic or question of the unit and the relationships between the groups they have created.

As they do so, they are activating background but also building it—since the pictures provide information and since some students will know what others do not and will share it during the process.

Photo Galleries

Create a gallery (actually or virtually) of photographs relevant to a reading (e.g., WPA photos from the Depression before reading *Roll of Thunder, Hear My Cry*). Students then examine the photos, addressing questions like these:

Who are these people?

What is their situation?

When were these photos taken?

What different groups are involved?

What are the problems/challenges/goals of each group?

As they do this, students are using visual cues to make inferences, building background knowledge, and helping each other build schema that will assist them as they move forward to read this Depression-era book.

A Class Scrapbook

Students find or take photos of power relations, friendship, or whatever the theme of a unit is, then bring these in and share and explain how they relate to the essential question. Or students can engage in video clubs, watching videos at home that pertain to the unit at hand and provide background knowledge to the class that will be useful throughout the unit. (All of these activities are thoroughly described in Wilhelm, 2012b.)

3. Activate Existing Schema

In the textual examples we shared earlier in the chapter, we counted on your having the necessary background knowledge. All we had to do was activate it. We did so by simply telling you or suggesting to you the topic of the reading ("In 1492 . . ."). Often, a text requires deeper and more complex conceptual understandings—perhaps understandings you as the reader do not yet possess. But if you think students already have the necessary prior knowledge in place then you can create an activity that will allow them to access it.

Writing Before Reading

One way of activating existing schematic background knowledge is through autobiographical writing before reading. In his study of the impact of autobiographical writing before reading, White (1995) used the following prompt to introduce a story that turned on whether a parent's advice was good or not:

> Most parents hope to teach their children what life is all about. They want to prepare their kids for life's possibilities, for life's pitfalls, for life's activities, for important decisions. First, describe a parent you think is a "good teacher." What does a parent need to be like in order to be a good teacher? Be as specific as possible and remember to write about parents *you know*. Second, describe a parent who's a bad teacher. What makes a parent a bad teacher? Again, be specific and write about parents that you yourself are acquainted with. (p. 184)

White found that the students who had done the kind of writing called for in this prompt were less apt to make off-task responses in subsequent class discussions. But more important, they were significantly more likely to comprehend, make inferences about character's traits, and analyze the development of character instead of merely focusing on the surface details of characters.

Such prompts as this are different from many generic journal topics in that they are far more developed. We've found that the more elaborated a prompt, the more elaborated are our students' responses. The key to the development of prompts is to identify a crucial conceptual issue in a text that you think students already have experience with and then detail what you want them to write about, encouraging them to develop and justify their thoughts.

Imagine that you plan to teach *Of Mice and Men*. (We use canonical literary examples in the hope that they're familiar to most of our readers.) One way into the book might be through the issue of friendship. You could write a prompt such as "Explain what you think makes a good friend." But we think you'd be far more successful with something like the following:

> Sometimes friends face difficult decisions about how they can best support each other in difficult times. Think of a friendship that you've experienced or observed in your life, read about, or seen in a movie or on TV when one friend was in some kind of trouble and the other had to figure out what to do to support or assist that friend. Describe the situation and explain some choices that the friend could have made to help the friend who was in trouble. Explain why the friend chose to do what he or she chose to do and whether you agree with that decision.

You haven't cued any particular response, but you are forcing students to think hard about the relevant issue. If they do this thinking, they'll have a rich response to connect to the issues in *Of Mice and Men*. If they share their responses with each other, they will be building a deep, multi-perspective schema around the issue of friendship and its challenges.

Once students write, it's up to you how you use that writing, though if you want students to share, make sure to tell them in advance. We found that the writing itself was often enough to activate the relevant schema, but we encourage you to return to the prompts during discussion, asking, for example, how an author or character would have responded to the prompt the students wrote about.

Surveys and Opinionnaires

If you know the work of George Hillocks and his students (see Hillocks, 2011), you've probably encountered opinionnaires. Opinionnaires are simply sets of controversial statements that you ask students to agree or disagree with (or strongly agree, agree, disagree, strongly disagree). Say that you are going to teach *Of Mice and Men* and you want to activate what students know about friendship, dreams, ambitions, and the morality of people's actions. You could give them an opinionnaire like the one in Figure 3.1.

Depending on your students' needs and your instructional context, you could focus on a single issue, for example, by adding three or four more statements about friendship. Or you could add statements that focus on still other themes—say, statements that might help students understand the causes of Curley's wife's loneliness and her responses to that loneliness. If you have trouble coming up with statements, you can look for quotes about the concept under consideration and ask students to rank them from the one they agree with most to the one they disagree with most. Here are five quotes on friendship taken from BrainyQuote:

> True friends stab you in the front.
>
> —Oscar Wilde

> A friend is someone who gives you total freedom to be yourself.
>
> —Jim Morrison

> What is a friend? A single soul dwelling in two bodies.
>
> —Aristotle

> A true friend is one who overlooks your failures and tolerates your success!
>
> —Doug Larson

> All you need to do to be my friend is like me.
>
> —Taylor Swift

When we use opinionnaires, we typically have students fill them out individually and then discuss them in small groups and then in large groups. We often ask students to choose one quote or statement that particularly resonated with them and to tell a personal story that illuminates or justifies their strong feelings. Once again, we encourage you to reuse the opinionnaires again and again, by asking students to fill them

OF MICE AND MEN OPINIONNAIRE

NAME: _____ DATE: _____

1. A true friend is willing to take any risk to help out a friend in need.

SA	A	D	SD

2. The best friendships are usually between people who are pretty similar.

SA	A	D	SD

3. People can achieve their dreams if they want them enough.

SA	A	D	SD

4. Everyone has an equal chance to succeed.

SA	A	D	SD

5. It's okay to take the law into your own hands if you have a good reason.

SA	A	D	SD

6. People are mostly worried about themselves.

SA	A	D	SD

Figure 3.1

out from other perspectives—for example, of authors or characters or historical figures from their subsequent readings.

Box 3.1 summarizes the steps of the process we have used to activate students' existing schema.

Process for Activating Kids Existing Schema

1. Choose which kind of activity is suitable for your kids and the text.

2. Have students respond individually.

3. Have students share their responses in small groups.

4. Draw on students' responses again and again in discussions of the text.

5. Have students engage in the activity from other perspectives.

Box 3.1

4. Develop and Build New Schema

Sometimes the text you want students to read will have a central concept that you're not sure your students have experience with or have thought seriously about. In such cases, your frontloading work will have to *develop* new schema rather than *activate* existing ones. Below we describe several ways you can do this.

Using Simulated Texts

When students don't have robust schema in place, opinionnaires may not be as fruitful as what we, following Langer (2001), call simulated texts. Simulated texts are texts that teachers develop that are designed to focus students' attention on a particular conceptual issue or strategy. Our focus in this chapter has been conceptual understandings, so we'll continue in that vein, taking up the use of simulated texts for strategy instruction next chapter. (We need to emphasize that if students don't have the strategic competence to read a text, then the best time to introduce and practice a needed strategy is *before* they read that text.)

Imagine that you're planning to teach *Julius Caesar*. One central issue that the play takes up is what constitutes the moral use of power. In thinking about that issue, we've come to understand that the dimensions of that issue include the following:

- What was the person's goal in striving for power?

- What are the means by which power was achieved?

- What are the results of the use of power?

Because we didn't think that students would have done much serious thinking about this issue, we developed a set of simulated texts to force them to think about those three questions (see Figure 3.2).

In writing the scenes, we tried to manipulate the three dimensions of using power in different ways. Joseph, for example, was moral but his morality may have had very negative consequences for the people of his country. Ivan came to power immorally but to good effect. If the simulated texts work, students will have to articulate their tacit understandings of power. The activity itself builds schema about the use of power and can help students connect to real-world examples, thereby expanding their schema. And once they have done so, they can apply these new schema to their reading. The process we suggest for using simulated texts to develop schema is much the same as the one we suggested for activities designed to activate existing schema.

Using Drama/Action Strategies

Another way to develop students' new understandings is through the use of drama/action strategies. Imagine again that you're teaching *Julius Caesar* and want to use the issue of power as a way in. You could start such a unit by using a technique called "four corners" (Wilhelm, 2012a), posting the names of four characters from your previous unit in the corners of your room and asking students to go to the corner of the character they thought had the most power. Imagine students trying to decide between

APPROVE OR DISAPPROVE

||||||||||||||||||||||||||||||||||||||||||||||||||||||||||||||||||||||||||||||||||||||||||||||||||||||||||||||||||||||||||||||||||||||||||||||||||||

NAME: _____ DATE: _____

Each of the following scenarios describes someone who is in power. Rank the characters whose names are in bold based on your approval of their actions. Give a 1 to the person you most approve of and a 4 the person you least approve of. Be sure to note the reasons for your relative approval and disapproval since you will be sharing your rankings.

_____1. **Karen,** an elementary school principal, had always been involved in politics at the local level in a behind-the-scenes way. She was very effective at encouraging people not to accept how things were but always to try to make things better, something she always told her told her students and coworkers. So when she complained day after day about how she was ashamed to be represented by a senator from her own party who was accused of taking illegal campaign contributions, her coworkers said, "Well, do something about it." So she decided to see if she could get enough signatures to run against him in the primary. She didn't expect to win, but she thought that by running she could speak out about the importance of ethics. The whole school community chipped in, and the signatures were collected. And then the unexpected happened: The senator withdrew from the race because he was convicted. Karen was thrust into the spotlight. She didn't think she'd be elected, but people seemed to want to listen to her call to clean up politics. And then in an election surprise, she won a narrow victory. Now it was her turn to go to Washington. In the three years since Karen has been elected, she has attended every committee meeting and every legislative session. She regularly goes home to hold town hall meetings so she can do the best possible job reflecting her state's views when she votes. However, she has not introduced any legislation even though her state is suffering from severe economic problems, a contrast to the man whom she defeated who had introduced two or three significant pieces of legislation every year. In fact, money that had gone to her state was starting to go to other states that had more aggressive representatives.

_____2. **Joseph's** country was plagued by brutal and corrupt leaders. Although he and his family were well-off, he couldn't stand by to see the suffering of others. He began to meet with others who shared his dissatisfaction to discuss what they could do to bring new leadership to the country. It took courage to do so, for if the rulers knew what Joseph was doing, his life and the lives of his wife and children would surely be in danger. It wasn't long before the word got out, however, and Joseph felt he had to send his family away for their safety. They all left except for his oldest son, who wanted to stand beside his father. Joseph became more and more outspoken, even after his son was beaten to death by a gang Joseph knew was associated with the rulers. But the beating had an effect the rulers

Figure 3.2

||||||||||||||||||||||||||||||||||||||||||||||||||||||||||||||||||||||||||||||||||||||||||||||||||||||||||||||||||||||||||||||||||||||||||||||||||||

NAME: _____ **DATE:** _____

didn't anticipate. It caused so much anger among the people that massive demonstrations were held all over the country. Now it was the rulers who fled, leaving Joseph to lead his country. Joseph was uncomfortable with being looked upon as a leader without the benefit of an election so he immediately began plans for one. He realized that followers from the previous rulers still had most of the country's wealth and would provide stiff opposition. However, Joe felt that he couldn't seize their wealth or remove them from them from the country because those were the sorts of tactics that he opposed. And besides, he was confident that the people would support him and his party in any election because he and his party had liberated them. Because they were able to bribe so many voters, the followers of the previous regime won the election in a close race. Once they were in power again, they were even more brutal than the previous rulers were. Their first act was to throw Joseph into prison. But now the eyes of the world were on Joseph's country, and things would perhaps change.

_____ 3. **Sally** headed a group that took over a business that was failing. Many observers criticized the takeover because it involved working to depress the price of the company's stock, though everything that Sally and her colleagues did was completely legal. Lots of stockholders lost lots of money, but this enabled Sally and her colleagues to gain a majority interest in the company. And once she had it, she knew what to do. When Sally became president of the business, her first act was to fire all of the older employees because they were making the highest wages, even though she knew that because of their age most of these people would not be able to find new jobs. She also cut back on benefits. Within a year, the company was back on its feet. Sally kept the same policies in force, and soon the company was making an outstanding profit and was able to hire even more workers than they ever had before. Sally was rewarded with a $50 million bonus.

_____ 4. **Ivan** was the vice president of small country. He achieved his position because his oldest childhood friend was the enormously popular president. Ivan's primary responsibility was overseeing the country's social programs, and under his leadership his country's level of education had increased tremendously and its hunger had decreased tremendously. Initially, his friend the president had taken pride in Ivan's efforts, but as the years went on, the president became more and more concerned with accumulating personal wealth. He also became more and more jealous of Ivan's popularity. Because the president began to take money from social programs, the people began to suffer. One evening, Ivan poisoned the food of the president, who died a horrible death. Ivan came to power, and he immediately restored all of the money to the social programs. The country's situation continually improved under Ivan's leadership.

Father Capulet, Friar Lawrence, Romeo, and the Prince from *Romeo and Juliet*. Once students are positioned, ask the students in each corner to confer about what kinds of power their character possessed, where it came from, and how they used it. In their corners, students discuss why they thought that this character was more powerful than the other three. Conclude by using a drama technique called "radio show," going to each group and interviewing them as a radio reporter about why they thought their character was most powerful while the students listen. Students can move from their corner if they are convinced to do so. In these dramas, students will have to draw on textual evidence in just the ways that the CCSS call for.

Combining Visual and Dramatic Activities

Picture books provide a way to combine visual and dramatic activities. For example, Jeff has used the picture book of the Gullah Island folktale *Sukey and the Mermaid* (San Souci) as the basis of a story drama to introduce concepts like power or civil rights. In a story drama, the teacher reads a picture book (or other text) aloud and occasionally stops for all students to engage in short, spontaneous, and scriptless drama activities or action strategies to help them experience different perspectives and live through and reflect on the story. At the beginning of Jeff's story drama with *Sukey*, students complete short role-plays in the role of Sukey, her mother, her abusive stepfather, and a family friend. Through the course of the book, there are many more dramas so that every student eventually has the opportunity to play every major character once, allowing the students to experience each perspective. After doing so, the students discuss who has what kind of power, who is exercising power responsibly, and how each character could become more powerful and responsible by modifying his or her behavior or situation.

Next, students choose the roles of characters they think may possess or could develop some power to help Sukey (guidance counselor, teacher, preacher, social worker, police officer, et al.) and engage in a forum meeting where they brainstorm, in role, what power they have to help, how they might exercise that power, and the costs and benefits of exercising their power in that way.

Box 3.2 provides a summary of the approach we advocate when using dramatic activities.

Using Dramatic Activities

If you use dramatic activities make sure you do the following:

- Clearly establish the context in which the drama is to take place, explaining when, where, and why the characters are interacting.

- Design the drama so that all students get to play important roles.

- Provide opportunities to reflect on and extend the drama—for example, by debriefing discussion or by having students do in-role writing.

Box 3.2

5. Focus on a Meaningful Purpose or Inquiry

Creating clear and compelling *purposes* for learning and *contexts* that require and reward particular kinds of learning helps prepare students for success versus reacting to deficits. This is what cognitive scientists call *situated cognition* (Brown, Collins, & DuGuid, 1989) and Hillocks (1986, 1995) calls *environmental teaching*. This powerful idea is well known in educational research and cognitive science (see, e.g., Newman & Associates, 1996; Newman & Wehlage, 1995; Smith & Wilhelm, 2002, 2006): Everything from vocabulary growth to deep procedural and conceptual understandings like those required by the CCSS are best achieved when students understand the purpose and immediate possibilities for using what is learned in contexts of actual use, like those provided through the use of inquiry.

The CCSS are entirely procedural/strategic. That is, they delineate quite carefully the skills and strategies that students need to develop, but they mention content only tangentially. The Standards focus is on helping

//

It won't do any good
to simply assign
harder and more
complex texts—any
teacher knows that
this will only lead
to disaster.

kids to develop and apply the HOW—on cultivating and using profound ways of knowing, problem solving, and making meaning that are valued in the disciplines, higher education, and out in the world.

"Inquiry" is defined in cognitive science as the rigorous apprenticeship into disciplinary procedures and understandings (see Wilhelm, 2007). Although the CCSS documents claim not to endorse any particular instructional theory or methodology, our interpretation of the research is that by far the best way to reach the strategic demands of the CCSS is through inquiry approaches. Not only do inquiry models meet student needs for purpose and motivation (see Wilhelm, 2007; Wilhelm, Wilhelm, & Boas, 2008), they provide the kinds of robust instructional support that all learners, but particularly reluctant and struggling learners, need most but are rarely offered. Instead, these students typically receive instruction that lacks substance, relevance, and edge.

Many studies demonstrate the case for inquiry. Our favorite is the Restructuring Schools Study conducted by Fred Newman and his colleagues at the University of Wisconsin (Newman & Associates, 1996; Newman & Wehlage, 1995). Involving 23 schools and more than 2,300 students, the study demonstrates that learners have significantly higher engagement and achievement on challenging tasks when they learn in an inquiry environment. Moreover, the study establishes that inquiry practices have more positive impact on student performance than any other factor, including prior achievement and background.

Inquiry contexts are especially important because of the CCSS's emphasis on the reading of complex texts. It won't do any good to simply assign harder and more complex texts—any teacher knows that this will only lead to disaster. Once students are in the ZFD, rescue and rehabilitation are no longer possible.

So we need to explicitly teach conceptual, procedural/strategic, and genre knowledge in a purposeful problem-solving context. How do we accomplish this? See Box 3.3 for key things on which to focus.

Providing this kind of preparation is going to require some mighty sophisticated and responsive teaching. We'll have to provide ways for all students to move through their zone of proximal development using differentiation through different materials, methods, groupings, duration of instruction, and levels of support.

1. **Frame instruction with an essential question** such as "What makes a good friend?" or "What is the best use of power?" (See our unit in Chapter 7 for teaching "Letter From Birmingham Jail," which begins with an essential question. You can also see a more extensive discussion in Smith & Wilhelm, 2010, and Wilhelm, 2007.)

2. **Frontload challenging texts** by preparing students to read them, just as a coach prepares his or her team for a big game.

3. **Carefully sequence instruction.** This means teaching texts that provide the frontloading and preparation to read the *next*, increasingly more complex text that requires students to use more sophisticated iterations of the concepts, procedures, and genre they learned previously. In other words, we'll need to pair texts that speak to each other and equip students with the concepts and procedures necessary to the reading or writing the next one in the sequence.

4. **Teach inside of students' current zones of proximal development.**

FOUR KEYS TO SUCCESSFUL INQUIRY INSTRUCTION

Box 3.3

Pulling It All Together

What does it look like to apply all this in the classroom? What follows is a brief description of an inquiry unit that Jeff teaches that includes an essential question, effective frontloading, and carefully sequenced instruction, all while teaching in the students' zones of proximal development.

For many years, Jeff has taught or helped to teach a *Romeo and Juliet* unit (for a complete description of the unit, see Wilhelm, 2007). Rather than thinking about the text alone, he now reframes this unit with a question:

What makes and breaks relationships?

This turns the unit into an inquiry, into a real problem to be solved, a problem that is complex and to which no one really knows a definitive answer. The unit begins with several frontloading activities to

motivate his students and to develop conceptual understandings that will help them have a meaningful transaction with the play.

One activity is an opinionnaire, designed along the lines we discussed earlier. It includes such statements as the following:

- Love means never having to say you are sorry.

- Teenagers cannot experience true love.

- It is better to have loved and lost than never to have loved at all.

Students are asked to indicate their level of agreement or disagreement, then to explain why they agree or disagree, using evidence and stories from their life experience. They then share these informal pieces of writing and discuss them.

As students read love songs and advice columns, informational text on relationships and evolutionary biology, fables about love, short poetry, and ultimately *Romeo and Juliet,* they return to the opinionnaire to explain the following:

- What they think the author or characters would say to each statement (making a claim)

- How they know what the author or character would say (providing evidence)

- How they know the evidence fits their claim (providing evidentiary reasoning or warranting)

Because love songs and advice columns are familiar to students, they are great places to start. Discussion of the songs can set the stage for reading the informational text. The informational text provides background knowledge that will help students evaluate the morals of the fables they read. Then they'll be ready to make inferences in short poetic texts before applying all that they've learned to reading the play.

Notice what is happening: Students are activating background interests and knowledge. They are also building their classmates' background knowledge as they set the terms of the debate, since they know and think different things. As they return to the survey after their readings, they are interpreting texts and deepening their understanding of the readings. And finally, they are practicing, practicing, practicing the basic moves of argumentation as they prepare for success on their final essay, an argument of literary interpretation.

This unit is good teaching (if we say so ourselves) because it involves preparing students for success on ever more complex texts and tasks. It provides the practice and assistance students need. Students develop knowledge throughout the unit and then apply what they learned in the culminating projects and writing assignments that conclude the inquiry. And what's true within units is also true across units. The cause/effect reasoning students have been practicing would certainly pay off in a unit built around a question like, "What allows/interferes with meaningful social change?"

The unit is also an example of extremely efficient teaching. In inquiry units, each text and assignment prepares students for subsequent texts and assignments. In essence, each reading is a pre-reading activity or a frontload for the next reading. Students are increasingly able to dive into the complex texts they encounter at the end of the unit because of the extended practice they received in thinking hard about the issues that are central to those texts. And, by the way, at the end of the nine-week unit, Jeff could show how he had addressed all 32 of the ELA anchor standards.

We realize an irony here. We critique Coleman for advocating how to teach, when the CCSS promise not to, yet we offer instructional suggestions ourselves. We hope, however, that you'll agree that our suggestions are grounded in research, that they are not based on caricatures, and that rather than being prescriptive, they are adaptable to meet the needs of different classrooms.

Moving Students to Independence

As he makes clear in "Bringing the Common Core to Life" (Coleman, 2011), one of Coleman's primary concerns is that students develop the ability to read independently without the support of a teacher. He's right about this; we do need to teach in ways that move students toward independence. But this, in part, may be where the crazy and dangerous "sink or swim" thinking about teaching comes from. *Assigning and assessing* is not teaching. Assigning challenging and complex text does not constitute instructing and supporting students to read in new and more powerful ways. Throwing somebody into the deep end of the pool is not

Assigning and assessing is not teaching. Throwing somebody into the deep end of the pool is not teaching that person to swim.

teaching that person to swim. In Michael and Jeff's (Smith & Wilhelm, 2002) interviews with boys, one of them made this point about teachers assigning but never assisting with challenging tasks: "It's like the teacher takes you out, throws you in the deep end of the pool, waits to see if you drown, and then marks it down in her gradebook." His complaint was not so much about being thrown into the deep end of the pool as about being thrown in without preparation, not being helped to be successful, and not being saved when he was in trouble.

The kind of teaching we are proposing and the use of frontloading we describe *does* create independent readers and writers who will flourish in life, college, and career as readers, writers, and thinkers. Of course, all teaching should be geared toward this kind of independence. Jerome Bruner invented the concept of scaffolding to capture this notion of how teaching should support and structure learning that, over time, becomes independent, internalized, and automatic. Just as we put up a scaffold to support and structure the construction of a wall or building, we must do the same for students when they are learning new concepts and strategies. Just as the scaffolding is taken away when the building can stand on its own, we do the same in our teaching.

If students don't need scaffolding and support, then they aren't learning anything new; they are doing what they already know how to do, stuck in their zone of actual development. Learning the new requires accessing or building resources, then applying them in new ways to the new challenge. This process requires teaching and assistance over time. This is why frontloading, which activates and builds resources and begins to create the instructional scaffold, is so essential to reading the complex texts and mastering the complex strategies required by the Core.

Here's an example: Jeff has often used group reading strategies such as literature circles in his classes. He experiments a lot with different roles, depending on what he is trying to help his kids do that is new to them, so he might have a "symbol seeker" or "narrator reliability judge" among his literature circle roles if these are strategies he is teaching at that time and wants students to practice. However, good readers don't play just one role; they play many different roles simultaneously: They visualize, they monitor comprehension, they learn vocabulary in context, they question, and they orchestrate all of this. The roles of visualizer, monitor, vocabulary maven, questioner, and discussion director are meant to isolate one of the roles so that it can be focused on and mastered. The group, as a whole, operates as one reader playing all the different roles of an expert reader. The goal is, over time, to have students internalize all the roles of expertise so that they can use them all independently. The literature circle is therefore a temporary scaffold. The goal is to make the scaffold obsolete and unnecessary because the learner is independent and no longer needs it.

So how do we scaffold, support, and lead students to do their own frontloading? One way to think about this is to consider how we, as expert adult readers, frontload our own reading. Here's an example: Jeff's book club met just last night and discussed Jim Holt's *Why Does the World Exist?* They also finalized their next book choice: Joseph Stiglitz's *The Price of Inequality*. Now, the new book was chosen in part because the group members have a prior interest in the topic, so that interest was activated. The group discussed their thinking about the topic of inequality (as they have on many occasions over time), which activated prior knowledge but also built on it because some group members knew things about the topic and the book that the rest did not. Gregor passed the book around and all flipped through it, making different remarks. The group recalled that Stiglitz had given a speech at Boise State University in 2007 that several of the group had attended. Each recounted a memorable anecdote from that speech. Jeff, for example, recalled how Stiglitz had so completely and correctly predicted the burst of the housing bubble and the banking crisis that caused so much trouble very shortly after Stiglitz's speech.

That evening, Wita sent the group a review of the book along with her comments. And Debra followed up by sending the URL for a blog that Stiglitz moderates.

Jeff, for one, bookmarked the URL, read several of the articles, and glanced through several more.

What was the group doing? They were preparing each other for success! They were frontloading in highly independent and interdependent ways that activated and built interest, that activated and built background, and that prepared each group member for engagement and success with the next reading. How did the group know to do this? They have internalized the strategies of expert frontloading and know how to prepare themselves for success.

Here's another example: Michael's daughters went to a high school that was very insistent that students not consult Wikipedia when they were writing research papers. Instead they were to use JSTOR to get relevant academic articles. We understand the impulse. After all, Wikipedia entries don't get professionally vetted for accuracy. But here's the problem: Michael's daughters couldn't read the JSTOR articles, all of which were written for an audience of experts. To help them do so, he'd read the abstracts of the articles and review these with his girls. And he might then go to Wikipedia himself (on the sly, of course) and share what he had learned with his daughters as a prelude to working through the articles with them. Sometimes, through Internet searches, he found a PowerPoint presentation from an introductory course on the topic of their papers or the excerpts or reviews of a relevant book he saw cited in the newspaper. Michael knew to do this because he makes similar moves all the time in his own reading. His book club recently read *The Nineteenth Wife*, a novel that centers on plural marriage and that features both Brigham Young and Ann Eliza Young as major characters. The Amazon reviews, a short article posted on the History Channel club, and Wikipedia all were useful in helping him develop background knowledge that made the book easier to understand and enjoy.

Here is another example of frontloading: When Deborah introduces literary theory to secondary students, she begins by showing them the old woman/young woman picture that we showed earlier to demonstrate there are multiple points of views on any subject. She then reads *The True Story of the Three Little Pigs by A. Wolf*, a children's story by Jon Scieszka that retells the familiar fairy tale from the wolf's point of view. Then students tell a family story from the perspective of at least two family members. Only when Deborah is convinced that she has laid adequate groundwork for students' understanding of multiple points of views does she introduce the theories themselves (Appleman, 2010).

How can we help our students practice and evaluate different ways of activating interest and accessing and building background so that they move toward independence as frontloaders, doing what expert readers do when they prepare themselves for success?

As teachers, we've argued that providing frontloading is a good and absolutely necessary thing to do when kids need it, but we also need to help them think independently about what background knowledge is necessary for them to read a text independently. Since this is so, we need

We need to help students think independently about what background knowledge is necessary for them to read independently.

to scaffold them into the process of doing so independently; we need to help mentor and monitor and transition them to doing so.

We can provide scaffolding by helping guide our students to preview a new book using a modified K-W-L format that adds in an all-important **H** for **HOW**. Using this, we ask our students to brainstorm:

- What do I already **Know (K)** about this topic?

- What do I **Want (W)** to know?

- **How (H)** can I find out what might be necessary to put me in the game (e.g., use Wikipedia, find an introductory PowerPoint course, find a relevant newspaper article, interview an expert or more knowledgeable person)?

- And finally, students can record what they have **Learned (L)** to placehold it for use during their reading.

This heuristic can be used with virtually every text.

We often have students brainstorm individually about what they know about the topic of a reading (research shows that doing this independently before sharing leads to more ideas) and then share in pairs and in the larger group. We then individually draw a web of the major topics and sub-topics, and then compare and combine these with webs created by their classmates. In this way, students are being asked to move toward independence with an easily internalized strategy for frontloading themselves.

Often, we ask our students after a preview, What do you need to know to be successful as a reader of this book? We then do a Google search or ask someone knowledgeable about conceptual questions we have; for procedural issues, we set up some practice (see the next chapter as well as Fredricksen, Wilhelm, & Smith, 2012, for examples of how this kind of practice works with writing narrative texts.)

We also ask students to list and consider the frontloading strategies that they've used before—in our own class or in other classes. We ask them to reflect on which ones worked best for them in specific cases and to consider how and why the frontloading strategies worked. We then ask students to identify what kind of frontloading strategies would work in the current case. For example, based on our use of opinionnaires, one group of students recently suggested looking up famous quotes about the reading/inquiry topic that could be referred to throughout a reading so that we could consider how this particular author was agreeing, disagreeing, or extending the ideas of others. (Jeff's book club could certainly do this for its next reading by looking up quotes about equality and inequality. These quotes could subsequently be used as response prompts in the next book club discussion.) Another group suggested thinking or writing about a personal connection to the topic or about related experiences. (Jeff's book club certainly told several personal stories about experiences with inequality.) Still another group of students suggested coming up with essential questions of their own to guide their reading.

In these various ways, the students were rehearsing how to move toward independence as frontloaders and as readers. In fact, during this activity, we were all engaged in taking down the scaffolding of provided frontloading, since students were transitioning to considering how to frontload themselves in highly flexible ways during their current and future readings.

In closing this chapter, we want to stress that one of the most exciting things about the CCSS is their focus on developing strategic tools for creating meaning and developing deep understanding and relevant real-world application. If we aren't teaching for understanding and application, then what in the heck are we teaching for? It's exciting to us that we can leverage the CCSS for college and career readiness as well as for citizenship readiness—for democracy and democratic living. That's a project worth working on, but it's going to take some excellent teaching.

And excellent teaching is about preparing students for success and helping students to continually outgrow themselves and move through their current zones of proximal development. Excellent teaching doesn't focus on correcting deficits in the midst of failure but, rather, cultivates strengths that lead to successful performances. Effective teaching is more about proactivity than reactivity.

Let's be proactive in taking on that challenge for the good of our students. That means doing lots of frontloading, practicing, and preparation for success and ignoring the crazy talk about sink-or-swim "teaching" coming from some of the CCSS camp.

Teaching for Transfer 4

Why Students Need to Learn How to Attend to *Any* Text

In our last chapter, we talked about the wrong-headed suggestion that teachers have students dive into texts without any sort of preparation. You might have noticed that our focus was on how pre-reading activities can help students develop the critical conceptual understandings that they need to have a meaningful transaction with particular readings. You may also have noticed that we did not take up Coleman's (2011) critique of what he calls "the third typical introduction" to a text: a mini-lesson on a strategy. We think that his critique in this case is grounded on his belief that effective instruction focuses on the teaching of *particular* texts, a belief manifested in Coleman's emphasis on text-dependent questions. Our purpose in this chapter is to explain why Coleman's exhortation that teachers focus on teaching individual texts in isolation rather than *approaches* to texts, or strategies that can be used with many texts, is misguided. We'll then explain approaches that are much more effective both in engaging kids in their present reading and preparing them for their future reading.

Where the Authors of the Standards Go Wrong About Closed-Ended, Text-Based Questions

An Analysis of David Coleman's Approach

Let's start by taking a close look at the approach Coleman advocates as exemplified by the plan Coleman shares for a three- to six-day (!) discussion-based lesson of the three paragraphs of the "Gettysburg Address." We'll be drawing on the written materials posted on the AchievetheCore.org website that were developed by Student Achievement Partners, an organization founded by David Coleman, Susan Pimentel, and Jason Zimba, all of whom were lead writers of the Common Core State Standards (CCSS; Achieve the Core, 2013). The version we used was last adjusted on November 26, 2013. You can also see Coleman talking about his instructional suggestions on PBS Learning Media (*The Gettysburg Address,* 2011). For the sake of brevity, we'll focus only on his suggestions for addressing the short first paragraph of Lincoln's address. Here's the text of that paragraph:

> Four score and seven years ago our fathers brought forth
> on this continent, a new nation, conceived in Liberty, and
> dedicated to the proposition that all men are created equal.

In teaching this text, Coleman and his colleagues first suggest that teachers ask students to read it independently, making sure teachers "refrain from giving background context or substantial instructional guidance at the outset" (Achieve the Core, 2013, p. 3). Then they suggest reading it aloud, not delivering it as an orator might but rather reading it "slowly and methodically" while students follow along. Then they suggest asking students to paraphrase the paragraph on their own. The lesson doesn't offer any mechanism for helping students to compose paraphrases, apparently assuming that students have already mastered this sophisticated strategy. Nor does the lesson suggest ways for students to share their paraphrases in any way. Instead, Coleman and his colleagues encourage teachers to move from asking students to write the paraphrases to asking five text-dependent questions:

1. What does Lincoln mean by "four score and seven years ago"? Who are "our fathers"?

2. What does **conceived** mean?

3. What does **proposition** mean?

4. What is he saying is significant about America? Is he saying that no one has been free or equal before? So what is new?

5. Sum up and gather what students have learned so far: have students summarize the three ways in which the nation is new. (pp. 4–5)

After each of these questions, the lesson provides instructional commentary. Here's what is written about question 1:

> Lincoln tells us *when* and by *whom* the country was founded. Let students know that these details will be addressed later more thoroughly. For now, though keep it simple—that "our fathers" founded the country some time ago. Point out to students that one important thing about reading carefully is that it helps to get a basic gist of a sentence before looking to understand every detail. (p. 4)

Why It Matters

Once again we think Coleman's suggestions are informed both by a caricature of the instructional approaches he criticizes and by a lack of knowledge of the research and theory that informs effective practice. Moreover, his instructional suggestions run counter to the CCSS themselves.

Let's start with a thought experiment. Imagine that you're in a book club that meets every other month. Imagine that you're leaving on vacation the day after a meeting at which the club's next reading was determined. "Great timing," you might think. "I can get the book read on vacation when I have some uninterrupted time." Now imagine the next book club meeting, seven weeks after you finished the book. Just how much will you remember? If you're like us, not so much.

Or another one: Imagine that you have a class full of the ultimate go-getters, kids who resolved to complete their summer reading assignment the moment school is let out in June. Now imagine you're writing your lesson plans for the first week of school. How much knowledge of the book can you count on? If your kids are like the kids we've taught, not so much.

We start with these thought experiments to make what we think is a critically important point: Our students are going to forget most of the details of most of the texts we teach them, if not by the time they leave our classes, then certainly by the time they start college. Look at the verbs that introduce the anchor standards for reading: *read closely, determine, analyze, interpret, analyze, assess, integrate, delineate and evaluate, analyze, read,* and *comprehend*. The CCSS emphasize *procedural, strategic* understandings. And they should, for those understanding are the ones that will be most useful for students in the future. If the CCSS stressed the content of particular texts, the anchor standards would instead be introduced with verbs like *remember, retell,* and the like.

The Importance of *Transfer*

The CCSS's emphasis on procedural knowledge is very much in line with what we know about best practice. Indeed the first recommendation made in the *Reading Next* report on adolescent literacy is that teachers provide "direct, explicit comprehension instruction" (Biancarosa & Snow, 2006, p. 4). In her more recent review of reading research, Goldman (2012) concludes that

> explicit teaching of strategies and their coordinated use is
> necessary for most students, especially when they are reading
> to learn. Students need opportunities to practice explicitly
> taught strategies and get feedback on their performance. (p. 96)

Goldman (2012) notes, however, that research paints a complex picture and that instruction needs to recognize that the strategies in which expert readers engage vary from discipline to discipline. That's why the issue of transfer is so important.

Transfer of knowledge means applying what one learns in one situation to problem solving in another. Sometimes problem-solving situations are similar. Transferring knowledge from one situation to a similar situation is what's called *near transfer*. For example, applying what one has learned about reading from instruction that made use of a fable to the reading of another fable by the same author would be near transfer. *Far transfer*, on the other hand, means applying knowledge learned in one context to a dissimilar context. For example, applying what one learned about reading from instruction that made use of a fable to one's reading of, say, a historical document would be far transfer. We can't anticipate the reading demands of the school and work contexts students will be entering after they graduate from high school. Nor can we anticipate the self-selected reading they will do. Therefore, encouraging far transfer has to be among our primary goals.

What position do the CCSS take on transfer? Cunningham (2013) makes an important argument. The Common Core authors' suggestion that instruction should be focused on the in-depth exploration of particular texts assumes that such instruction will lead to transfer. After all, he explains, "One of the 'key features' of the Common Core Reading Standards is 'the growth of comprehension'" (p. 140). Moreover, according to Cunningham,

> This growth is delineated [in the CCSS] in some detail:
> "Whatever they are reading, students must also show a
> steadily growing ability to discern more from and make
> fuller use of text, including making an increasing number
> of connections among ideas and between texts, considering
> a wider range of textual evidence, and becoming more
> sensitive to inconsistencies, ambiguities, and poor reasoning
> in texts." (p. 140)

But here's the kicker: According to Cunningham, "there is very little existing research" (p. 141) to support the assumption on which Coleman's teaching ideas are based.

What's worse, there's ample reason to believe that research backing Coleman up will not be forthcoming. In the most comprehensive review of research on transfer of which we're aware, Haskell (2000) points out that "despite the importance of transfer of learning, research findings over the past nine decades clearly show that as individuals, and as educational institutions, we have failed to achieve transfer of learning on any significant level" (p. xiii).

Why? As Perkins and Salomon (1988) explain, "A great deal of the knowledge students acquire is 'inert'" (p. 23), meaning that students

Transfer of knowledge means applying what one learns in one situation to problem solving in another. Encouraging . . . transfer has to be among our primary goals.

don't apply it in new problem-solving situations. Despite the research on the difficulty of transfer, Perkins and Salomon argue that teachers remain sanguine about its likelihood, relying on what they call the Little Bo Peep view of transfer; that is, if we "leave them alone" students will come to a new task and naturally transfer relevant knowledge and skills. David Coleman seems to subscribe to the Little Bo Peep theory.

So the bad news is that the instructional approach that Coleman models is unlikely to lead to the transfer of skills for most students. But there's some good news as well. Under certain *other* conditions, transfer is much more likely to happen. Haskell (2000) presents 11 conditions that foster transfer that we think can usefully be reduced to four:

1. If students have command of the knowledge that is to be transferred

2. If students have a theoretical understanding of the principles to be transferred

3. If a classroom culture cultivates a spirit of transfer

4. If students get plenty of practice in applying meaning-making and problem-solving principles to new situations

Haskell's (2000) summary of the research on transfer is remarkably similar to Byrnes's (2008) more recent formulation. Byrnes explains that

> transfer is more likely if students can (a) partially decontextualize skills and develop conditional knowledge about their application, (b) cast their knowledge in the form of principles, (c) develop a conceptual understanding of procedures, and (d) approach their learning in a mindful way. (p. 79)

Perkins and Salomon (1988) concur, arguing that cultivating a "mindful abstraction" of a strategy allows it to be moved from "one context to another" (p. 25). We think of it this way: Naming a skill or strategy makes the strategy *tool-ish* and not *school-ish*, for if you can name it, then you have tamed it. As a consequence, we think it's crucially important for teachers to help their student gain conscious control over their reading strategies, what's called *metacognition* in the research literature.

> The instructional approach that Coleman models is unlikely to lead to the transfer of skills for most students.

What we've seen so far is that Coleman's suggestion to emphasize instruction centered on learning from particular texts has no empirical support, flies in the face of an established body of knowledge on the effectiveness of teaching reading strategies, and does not take into account research on the conditions that foster transfer support.

At the risk of sounding like a late-night infomercial . . . *But that's not all.* We think Coleman's support of text-dependent questions is based on a caricature of actual teaching practice, a caricature at odds with what we know about classroom discussions of literature. Coleman seems to have two fundamental worries about the questions he suggests typify classroom discussion of texts. We'll summarize those worries and then explain why we think they are unfounded.

One of his worries is that teachers ask response-centered questions that encourage students to depart from the text. Here's how he puts it (all the following quotes come from the full transcript of Coleman's "Bringing the Common Core to Life," a presentation made for the New York Department of Education on April 28, 2011; see Coleman, 2011):

> Now, this may seem quite obvious to you, but let me tell you the results of an informal study we did of instruction in Vermont and Texas. Now, we were looking for two of the most dissimilar states possible, which is why we chose those two. And what we found was is a remarkable similarity between those two very different places and it was that 80% of the questions kids were asked when they are reading are answerable without direct reference to the text itself. Think about it, right? You're reading a text and you talk about the background of the text, or what it reminds you of, or what you think about it, or what you criticize or perhaps how you feel or react to it, or all sorts of surrounding issues—kids are genius at this—because anything to avoid confronting the difficult words before them is money. (p. 10)

We can see Coleman's first worry play out when he explains his suggestions for teaching King's "Letter From Birmingham Jail." Let's look at what he says about teaching paragraphs 15 to 21 of the letter. After providing a summary of those paragraphs and encouraging teachers to probe deeply King's argument in them, he says,

> [In] paragraphs 15 to 21 and following, [King] makes a distinction between just and unjust law. And some people have asked me impatiently about this exercise. When do we get beyond the letter? When do we get beyond to the broader issues of social injustice? Whether or not you believe in nonviolence, whether you believe in civil disobedience? I want to suggest a couple of things to you. The first principle is allow first the rich comprehension of exactly what King is doing. (p. 21)

Each of us spends lots of time with teachers and in schools, and we've never seen this kind of abandonment of the text. Indeed, our experience suggests that Coleman is creating a false binary. In our experience, teachers don't ask these questions as a way to avoid texts but rather as way get students *into* texts or to apply or critique what they've learned from them.

The Importance of Authentic Questions

Our second worry is how the authors of the Standards discuss the use of generic questions. Here's how Coleman and Pimentel (2012) put it in *Revised Publishers' Criteria for the Common Core State Standards in English Language Arts and Literacy, Grades 3–12*:

> Good questions engage students to attend to the particular dimensions, ideas, and specifics that illuminate each text. Though there is a productive role for good general questions for teachers and students to have at hand, materials should not over rely on "cookie-cutter" questions that could be asked of any text, such as "What is the main idea? Provide three supporting details." Materials should develop sequences of individually crafted questions that draw students and teachers into an exploration of the text or texts at hand. High quality text dependent questions are more often text specific rather than generic. That is, high quality questions should be

developed to address the specific text being read, in response
to the demands of that text. (pp. 6–7)

Once again, although we've seen a question like the one he asks above
on assessments, we haven't seen it in classroom discussions except on
occasion as the culmination of a series of other questions.

The informal study done by Coleman and his colleagues doesn't square
with our experience. Nor does it jibe with the very formal studies
that have been done about classroom discussions of texts by leading
researchers in our field. For example, Applebee, Langer, Nystrand, and
Gamoran's (2003) analysis of 20 seventh- to twelfth-grade classrooms
reports that what they call *open discussion*, defined as "more than 30
seconds of free exchange of ideas among students or between at least
three participants" which "usually begins in response to an open-ended
question about which students can legitimately disagree" (p. 707) aver-
aged 1.7 minutes per 60 minutes of class time. Say what you will about
the response-centered and generic strategy questions that Coleman critiques, they are undoubtedly open-ended.

In a more recent study (Elizabeth, Ross Anderson, Snow, & Selman,
2012), it was reported that

> in line with past researchers' findings that very high quality
> classroom dialogue rarely occurs (Applebee et al., 2003;
> Nystrand et al., 2003; Nystrand & Gamoran, 1991), we found
> no instances of accountable talk in our data set. The majority
> of student discussions predominantly featured students
> politely responding to teacher-directed questions without
> considering or acknowledging the thoughts, comments, or
> ideas of their peers. (p. 1230)

That is, they found no instances of classroom talk that holds students
"responsible for the integration of their own reasoning and knowledge with that of their peers" (p. 1220). Say what you will about the
response-centered and generic strategy questions, they at least have the
capacity to result in accountable talk, for students could certainly build
on the responses of their classmates as they seek to answer them.

A long-established body of research strongly suggests that we ought to worry about the patterns of discourse that typify school discussions of texts. But our worries should be about teachers' asking narrow and inauthentic questions that foster passivity, for such questioning does not lead to increased achievement on the complex literacy tasks the CCSS are designed to foster.

We don't want to be guilty of caricaturing Coleman's ideas, especially given our concern about the caricatures he offers. We don't think he wants passive students. In fact, he says in a video interview that he wants to ask teachers to ask questions that "deliver richly" (*Common Core in ELA/Literacy,* 2012). We recognize that he wants teachers to ask interesting sequences of text-based questions "so that we don't have to go outside the text for excitement," but we worry that the model instruction he provides doesn't enact what we know about best practice—that is, that students need opportunities to work together to grapple with authentic questions—and so would not achieve his goals.

In contrast to what we know about best practice, the text-dependent questions that Coleman provides as a model seem to us to enact the very patterns of discourse that so worry researchers who study classroom discussions of texts. As the instructional commentary on the "Gettysburg Address" makes clear, all of Coleman's questions have single correct answers. And take another look at his suggestions for teaching paragraphs 15 to 21 of King's letter. Students can't talk about the significance of King's ideas until they understand "exactly what King is doing." The "exactly" is quite telling we think. No room for even minor disagreements about King's rhetorical moves.

The questions Coleman suggests imply that reading is simply decoding factual information. Look back again at his suggestion to have students paraphrase the first paragraph of the "Gettysburg Address." Students' paraphrases might differ, but he doesn't suggest having students share or having them work together to refine either the initial version or their revisions. Look back at the questions he suggests. Which of them would foster the intellectual excitement that he seeks or deliver richly on the close analysis he wants to encourage?

Ironically, none of the questions would seem to get after what the anchor standards call for. Take a look at reading Anchor Standard 1:

> Our worry should be about teachers' asking narrow and inauthentic questions that foster passivity, for this will not lead to increased achievement.

1. Read closely to determine what the text says explicitly and to make logical inferences from it; cite specific textual evidence when writing or speaking to support conclusions drawn from the text.

Coleman's questions do indeed focus on the first infinitive in Anchor Standard 1, as they ask for students to determine what the text says explicitly. But we don't see any invitations to make inferences. And we don't see how his questions would create a context that would require students to support a conclusion. Indeed, as his instructional commentary after each question reveals, all of his questions have answers that have been long settled.

To the extent that our goal is to have students emerge with an understanding of the content of a particular text, it makes sense to ask the kinds of questions that Coleman suggests. If you accept that goal, it makes sense for discussions to be designed to bring students to *our* particular interpretation of the text under discussion. After all, we're trained readers. We're older. We've likely read the texts we're teaching many, many times while our students have only encountered them for the first time (more on this later). But that teacher-centeredness has huge consequences, consequences that will undermine our students' capacity to meet the rest of the reading anchor standards and much else that we value about reading.

Here's what Applebee and his colleagues (2003) conclude from their study:

> The approaches that contributed most to student performance on the complex literacy tasks that we administered were those that used discussion to develop comprehensive understanding, encouraging exploration and multiple perspectives rather than focusing on correct interpretations and predetermined conclusions. (p. 722)

But invoking a late night infomercial once again . . . *There's still more.* Centering instruction on text-dependent questions is also problematic because in asking them, the teacher has done most of the interpretive work by noticing what aspects of the text are worth asking about. Rabinowitz (see Rabinowitz, 1987; Rabinowitz & Smith, 1998) has convinced us that

As Coleman's instructional commentary after each question reveals, all of his questions have answers that have been long settled.

such noticing is at the very heart of interpreting texts. Rather than drawing students' attention to what they should think about, we need to teach them how to learn to notice particular textual features that will help them think about texts and their meanings on their own.

Once again, we find it ironic that the approach Coleman advocates seems to us to be very much at odds with the CCSS themselves. Take a look at reading Anchor Standards 4 and 5:

> 4. Interpret words and phrases as they are used in a text, including determining technical, connotative, and figurative meanings, and analyze how specific word choices shape meaning or tone.

> 5. Analyze the structure of texts, including how specific sentences, paragraphs, and larger portions of the text (e.g., a section, chapter, scene, or stanza) relate to each other and the whole.

You can't interpret or analyze aspects of a text unless you have decided what's worth interpreting or analyzing.

So the text-dependent questions that Coleman endorses are not likely to rescue students from unfocused discussions that don't require them to read or from bland cookie-cutter questions that don't require them to think. Indeed, we have no good evidence that supports Coleman's assertion about how common such discussions are. Moreover, the kinds of discussions he promotes are likely to result in a sterile classroom atmosphere that undermines student learning because they foster dependence on teachers' interpretation and substitute playing guess-what's-on-the-teacher's-mind for collaborative and accountable talk about authentic questions. Indeed, a wealth of research suggests that we don't have too few closed-ended, text-based questions but, rather, too many.

How You Can Get It Right: Six Strategies That Increase Comprehension and Independence

So what to do? Below we describe in detail six teaching suggestions that are consistent with the research and theory we've presented above.

GENERAL RULES OF NOTICE

Remember to notice and interpret the meaning of the following:

General Rules of Notice

Titles. Pay attention to titles! Does this title tell us who to pay attention to or something we should know about a character or what will happen to her?

Beginnings

Climaxes/Key Details

Extended Descriptions

Changes in . . .

- Direction
- Setting
- Point of View

- Repetition
- Surprises and Ruptures
- Endings

Rules of Notice for Characters

Names and Nicknames. The names and particularly the nicknames of characters are almost always important and reveal something about the characters.

Introductions. Pay attention when characters are introduced!

Problems. Pay attention to any problem the character might have or a challenge they are facing.

Actions. Pay attention to characters' typical activities as well as actions they take.

Physical Description. Pay attention to characters' physical features and how they are described.

Clothing. Pay attention to what characters wear.

Way They Talk/Language They Use. Think about what dialects, tone, correctness, and language use say about characters.

Typical Setting or Surroundings. Where do they hang out, how do they decorate their room, where do they feel comfortable or uncomfortable?

Friends or People They Hang With. Notice what company do they choose to keep.

What Others Say About Them. Think about what people who know the character say about him or her.

Tastes/Likes/Dislikes. Pay attention to the particular tastes, attitudes, feelings, beliefs, soapbox opinions, or antipathies the character expresses

Character Thoughts. Think about what we learn about a character from his or her private thoughts, fears, desires?

Character Changes. Changes in a character are always important! If a character changes, it is for a reason, and the author wants us to figure out what the reason is. This will probably have something to do with the author's generalization or theme of the story.

Source: Based on the work of Peter Rabinowitz in *Before Reading.*

Available for download from **www.corwin.com/uncommoncore**.

Figure 4.1

1. Teach Students to Notice and to Ask Their Own Questions

If we want students to be independent interpreters of texts, we need to help them understand how to ask their own questions rather than wait for teachers to ask theirs. All of us have been significantly influenced by Peter Rabinowitz's *Before Reading* (1987, also available online) as a resource to help us understand how experienced readers work to understand text. Rabinowitz provides a wonderfully rich account both of why we notice what we notice (what he calls rules of notice) and how we make sense of what we notice (what he call rules of configuration and signification.) We think his book is must reading, but you can get a flavor of the kind of work he does by taking a look at the chart Jeff (Wilhelm, 2013c) developed on the basis of Rabinowitz's book (see Figure 4.1, p. 130).

But, of course, Rabinowitz's (1987) analysis is not the only one that's available. Lesley Rex and David McEachen (1999) coauthored an article titled "'If Anything Is Odd, Inappropriate, Confusing, or Boring, It's Probably Important': The Emergence of Inclusive Academic Literacy Through English Classroom Discussion Practices" that details how McEachen integrated regular-track students into a class for gifted and talented students by helping them understand and apply the rule of notice expressed in the title, a rule that was at the center of the interpretive work they did together. More recently Beers and Probst (2013) have written about what they call signposts for noticing in narrative texts: contrasts and contradictions, aha moments, words of the wiser, memory moments, and others.

Or you can develop your own. Lauren Lee, a teacher at Oak Park and River Forest High School in Illinois, developed a unit in which she and her students worked to develop a catalog of the "weird authorial behaviors" (e.g., undue attention to seemingly insignificant details, repetition, echoing the title) that signal to the reader that a symbol is being introduced.

See Box 4.1 for our typical process for teaching students to apply rules of notice independently.

Teaching Students to Apply Rules of Notice Independently

1. Determine what rules of notice to focus on.

2. Illustrate how to apply the focal rule or set of rules through a think-aloud or some other kind of modeling.

3. Give students extended practice in applying the rules on their own on some sensible sequence of texts (e.g., short texts in which the application of a rule is obviously called for, to a longer text in which the invitation to apply the rule is less obvious).

4. Track students' work with the rule in some fashion or another, or even better, have them track their own work with the rule through various kinds of formative assessments that they can share with each other and with you to reinforce the learning.

5. Engage students in considering the extent to which the rule is applicable to other types of texts.

Box 4.1

Another way to help students ask their own questions rather than rely on a teacher's questions is to teach them some kind of questioning taxonomy. We're most familiar with Hillocks's reading inventory (Hillocks & Ludlow, 1984), an empirically validated hierarchy of seven question types.

Fitzpatrick (2005, p. 149) explains Hillocks's seven question types and illustrates each with an example from William Carlos Williams's powerful short story, "A Question of Force," about a doctor forcing a child to open her mouth to reveal her diphtheria. See Figure 4.2.

SEVEN QUESTION TYPES

Use the question levels to help you think hard about a passage.

Level	Reading Inventory Questions	What a Reading Level Response of This Type Does
1. Basic stated information	• How well does the doctor know this family? • How long has the child been sick? • What does the doctor need in order to do to find out if the child has diphtheria?	Restates important information: • Who, what, where, or when • Character information • Action
2. Key details	• Why do they suspect that she has diphtheria? • What does the doctor's exam reveal? • What are the effects of diphtheria infection?	Distinguishes between important and irrelevant information. Identify facts that have the greatest impact on the plot: • Changes in the course of the story • Big revelations
3. Stated relationships	• Why don't the parents speak much at first? • Why does the father's participation make it hard to complete the exam? • What does the narrator say are his reasons for continuing with the exam?	Re-explains a connection stated in the text. • Cause or effect • Similarity or contrast • Reason why
4. Simple implied relationships	• Why is the child so resistant to being examined? • How does the mother contribute to the child's fear and discomfort?	Explains the implication of a particular statement in the text: • Unstated cause or effect • Unstated judgment of a character • Motivation for a single action
5. Complex implied relationships	• How does the doctor's attitude toward the child change throughout the story? What details and/or examples from the story support your answer?	• Demonstrates the implied connection between several details from various places in the text. • Generalizes about a major change in a character. • Generalizes about implied comparisons or contrasts.
6. Author's generalization	• How does the story suggest what causes might bring otherwise reasonable people to use violence against a child? What details and/or examples from the story support your answer?	• Supports a generalization about the world using evidence from the text. • Applies the generalizations suggested in the text to the world. • Demonstrates the implications of the author's representation of the world.
7. Structural generalization	• Explain the significance of the title of the story. What details and/or examples from the story support your answer?	• Supports a generalization about the purpose of literary elements used in the story. • Explains how the author's generalization is supported by the structure of the story. • Connects literary techniques to the generalization about the world.

Figure 4.2

Fitzpatrick (2005) tells his students to use the question levels to help them think hard about a particular passage. The payoff for that hard thinking is the subsequent class discussions. As he explains, the question levels "work *in service of* more satisfying, better informed reading experiences with texts selected to resonate with important life themes" (pp. 148, 150). That satisfaction comes primarily in rich discussions of levels 5, 6, and 7 and in relating the results of those discussions to students' lives and to other readings they have done.

Once again, a variety of alternatives would let you and your students do similar work. You're probably familiar with Bloom's taxonomy of educational objectives, which describes six levels in the cognitive domain: knowledge, comprehension, application, analysis, synthesis, evaluation. Bloom's taxonomy is now revised (Krathwohl, 2002) to focus, like the Core, on learner strategies or procedures of meaning making:

1. **Recognizing and remembering:** Think rules of notice!

2. **Understanding:** Including summarizing, inferring, exemplifying, comparing, and explaining

3. **Analyzing:** Including interpreting, classifying, differentiating, attributing, organizing, and structuring

4. **Applying**

5. **Evaluating**

6. **Creating**

The final three levels are all critical inquiry extensions in which students go beyond the text to transfer strategies in service of critiquing and creating their own meaning independently.

To achieve the Core and move students through Bloom's taxonomy, one option is to teach students question stems associated with each level. Another is to teach them Raphael's (1982) QAR (Question–Answer Relationship) or any other taxonomy of questions that you think would be useful. The process for doing so is the same as teaching students rules of notice, highlighted in Box 4.2.

Teaching Students to Apply Questions Independently

1. Determine what taxonomy of questions to focus on.

2. Illustrate how to apply the central question(s) through a think-aloud or some other kind of modeling.

3. Give students extended practice in applying the questions on their own on some sensible sequence of texts (e.g., short texts in which the application of a question is obviously called for, to a longer text in which the invitation to apply the question[s] is less obvious).

4. Track students' work with the questions in some fashion or another, or even better, have them track their own work with the questions through various kinds of formative assessments that they can share with each other and with you to reinforce the learning.

5. Engage students in considering the extent to which the questions are applicable to other types of texts.

Box 4.2

Yet another way to cultivate students' understanding of what's worth noticing is to teach them the assumptions underlying various critical theories and engage them in using those theories as lenses when they read. Deborah (Appleman, 2009) details how to do so with a wide variety of students. You'll see this approach in greater detail in our lesson on "Letter From Birmingham Jail" in Chapter 7, but for now we'll just offer this: By looking at texts from a variety of critical perspectives—including gender, social class, reader response, biographical and historical criticism, and formalism—students can learn to find different meaning and significances, depending on the critical perspective they adopt. By trying on various lenses, students develop an understanding of the kinds of noticing expert readers do. They are able to create multiple interpretations of a single text. They also get a sense of which lens is most useful for what kinds of texts in what kinds of contexts—all skills of expert, independent readers.

2. Combine Maxi-Lessons on
Strategies With Text-Specific Application

We agree with Coleman on one score: Single mini-lessons on strategies are unlikely to be very useful. Reading strategies are complex, and learning something complex takes time. Anders Ericsson's seminal research on the necessity of directed and focused practice for the development of expertise, which we have already mentioned, makes this clear. Michael and Jeff (Smith & Wilhelm, 2010) and Deborah (Appleman, 2010; Appleman & Graves, 2012) have published books relatively recently explaining our ideas for teaching interpretive strategies for the reading of literature in ways that provide the necessary kind of practice to develop transfer and conscious competence. You can see our ideas spun out in great depth there, and here we'll provide two illustrations.

As we've noted, Coleman critiques cookie-cutter questions such as "What is the main idea?" But take a look at what he says when he models how he would teach King's "Letter From Birmingham Jail." In discussing the first question, he proposes asking, on the basis of the first paragraph and the first paragraph alone, "What can you tell about the letter that King received?" He notes, "It is almost always helpful when an author is making an argument to get a sense of what is the argument they [*sic*] are pushing against" (*Close Reading of Text,* 2011). We agree. But it's important to note that thinking about the argument a writer is pushing against to refine your understanding of the author's own argument sounds like a generic strategy, doesn't it? And if doing so works across texts, then doesn't it make sense to help students learn how to do it better?

Imagine having students work in groups on the activity in Figure 4.3.

This preparation will make it far more likely that more students will be able to respond to the first question Coleman suggests posing about King's "Letter," but more important, it makes it far more likely that they'll consider what an author is writing against *whenever they encounter an argument.* Indeed, we'd argue that after such preparation it would make sense to ask students to posit the ideas the Lincoln is speaking against in the "Gettysburg Address" rather than beginning the lesson on this text, as Coleman suggests, with a paraphrase.

WHO'S ON THE OTHER SIDE?

One great way to help understand the primary ideas an author is trying to communicate is to think about what ideas the author appears to be writing against. Imagine that each excerpt below is the beginning of an editorial or speech that relates to school in some way or another. Think about what ideas the author is writing against. On the basis of who the author is writing against, discuss what ideas the author might be writing *for*.

1. The most powerful lessons anyone learns are learned from living, not from reading books. If we want students to be truly educated we have to give them time to explore, to play sports, to go to museums, to be with friends.
   - What ideas might the author be writing against?
   - What ideas might the author be writing for?

2. Schools should be about more than reading, writing, and 'rithmetic. They should also be about learning to work with others different from ourselves. A class of kids with similar abilities in math may indeed get a chapter or two more done than one that has kids of differing abilities, but at what cost?
   - What ideas might the author be writing against?
   - What ideas might the author be writing for?

3. High school is hard enough for kids without having to worry about not having the "right" kind of jeans or the trendiest shirt or blouse.
   - What ideas might the author be writing against?
   - What ideas might the author be writing for?

4. "First-period English class, 7:40 a.m. Most of the ninth-grade students stare glassy-eyed at their teacher. Two lay their heads on the desk." From "Sleep and Adolescents," by Peg Dawson (2005, p. 1).
   - What ideas might the author be writing against?
   - What ideas might the author be writing for?

5. "Students in the United States spend much less time in school than do students in most other industrialized nations, and the school year has been essentially unchanged for more than a century." (Marcotte & Hansen, 2010)
   - What ideas might the author be writing against?
   - What ideas might the author be writing for?

6. More and more United States prisons resemble nursing homes with bars, where the elderly and infirm eke out shrunken lives. (Fellner, 2013)
   - What ideas might the author be writing against?
   - What ideas might the author be writing for?

7. Think back on the answers you've provided. Explain as best you can how you came to your conclusions.

Now try applying what you've learned to a new situation.

Figure 4.3

Although the question is a generic (and hence transferable) one, it requires careful attention to the text to answer. But, as we said, in addition to requiring students to attend carefully to the text, it is teaching them something important about how experienced readers do their work.

Our second illustration seeks to cultivate even further transfer. To illustrate how one might make connections between literary and nonliterary texts, we'll share an activity that we developed for the reading of literature and see how it could also be applied to teaching the "Gettysburg Address."

The question, "What is the setting of this story?" is a generic question that asks students to employ the strategy of making inferences. It probably does even less work than "What is the main idea?" if in an answer students just quickly respond with the story's location. But setting is far more complex, for different texts focus on different levels of setting:

- **Microlevel:** Stories that focus on a *microlevel* of setting focus on the most local situation. In a story set in a school, the micro-level might be a particular classroom.

- **Mesolevel:** Stories that focus on the *mesolevel* take a slightly larger view. In a story set in a school, the mesolevel could be the entire school or maybe the community in which the school is located.

- **Macrolevel:** Other stories may take a still larger view, one that invites readers to think about larger social systems. For example, the most significant level of setting for a story set in a school could be the state of education in the United States in regard to its testing and accountability measures or gender relations or some such.

- **Dimensions of settings:** Settings also have different *dimensions*. Dimensions of setting include the following:
  o Physical space
  o Temporal space
  o Social dimension
  o Psychological dimension

> Teaching students how to question teaches them something important about how experienced readers do their work.

In some stories, the actual physical space is most important. In some stories, the temporal dimension is more crucial. In others, it's the social or psychological dimension.

Imagine working with students to understand those levels and those dimensions. A think-aloud would once again be useful as would working with the class to examine short texts. Comic strips are an efficient way to help students see how texts differ in terms of the significance of the levels of setting. For example, we analyzed the comics section of the *Philadelphia Inquirer* on the day we drafted this section of the book:

- *Dustin* and *Sherman's Lagoon* both seem to us to focus on the macrolevel by making a reference to the NSA.

- *Pickles* and *Jump Start* focus on the microlevel as they emphasize characters' relationships.

- *Edge City* seems to us to focus on the mesolevel as the characters' relationship is nested in one character's taking on a new hobby with all of its attendant demands.

Other strips aren't so clear to us and so would be great fodder for discussion.

With that preparation on micro- and mesolevels settings, the class could read a little story like "New Friends" (see Figure 4.4) that Michael (Smith & Wilhelm, 2010) wrote.

Now imagine giving students the following activity (see Figure 4.5) to work on individually and then in small groups.

As the culmination of this text-dependent activity, we would bring the class together for discussion and ask these two generic strategy-focused questions:

- What level of setting is most important in this story?

- What dimension of setting is most important in this story?

After that discussion, it's important to help students cultivate near transfer by asking them the very same question about the next narrative that they read. Think about asking the level of setting that's most important in, say, *Of Mice and Men*. Is that story more about a particular friendship or about social class? Once students have had enough experience thinking with the different levels and dimensions, asking the generic questions and probing for evidence will be enough to generate rich text-based discussions, at least for texts in which the answers are somewhat problematic.

Now imagine working to cultivate far transfer by asking them to consider the most important level of setting in the "Gettysburg Address." Is Lincoln speaking primarily to the people assembled at the battlefield, or does he have a larger audience in mind? Once again, in order to respond, students have to pay careful attention to the text.

In short, students must practice over time to develop transferable strategies that they can apply to new situations. They also need conscious control of the concepts and procedures they are using. Finally, they need to experience the payoff for developing that control by experiencing an increased ability to engage with an increasingly wide variety of texts.

One note before we go on. We imagine how David Coleman might object to what we've written here. *See, they're substituting the reading of quasi-texts (the introductory sentences in the first activity and Michael's story in the second) for reading texts that matter.* Guilty as charged. But we want to stress that working with texts designed to help students hone particular targeted strategies, what Langer (2001) calls *simulated texts*, are enormously efficient. Coleman advocates three days of instruction on the "Gettysburg Address." Working on the seven excerpts we provided, then, gives students a month's worth of practice that will enable them to orient themselves to arguments in about a day of class time. Strategy instruction done correctly doesn't cost time, it saves time. Little wonder that Langer found that teachers who beat the odds in terms of their students' performance on standardized tests focused both on developing specific strategies and on integrating the use of those strategies into meaningful holistic activity.

Students must practice over time to develop transferable strategies that they can apply to new situations.

"NEW FRIENDS" TEXT

Every four years around the time of the Olympics, the Department of Education would put on a Middle School Olympics where kids from around the world would come together to showcase their talents. The event lasted three weeks.

Every participating school could send five students. But each student had to have a different talent or interest. Joe felt fortunate to be selected to represent the athletes from his school. The other students who were going were Marcy, who played the cello; Zack, who was really into manga; Sharon, who starred in all the school plays; and Ed, who was a complete braniac.

Once the kids were selected, they had to get together for lots and lots of orientation. Joe never would have hung out with any of the other kids who were going. Not that he had anything against them. At his school, though, athletes stuck with athletes pretty much. Well, really basketball players stuck with basketball players. That was the big sport. He knew some of the other kids resented basketball and he could see why. Some of his teachers even seemed to favor him because he was the star. His mom, though, always kept his head from getting too big. She seemed to get along with everyone. Sometimes she took him to the African American neighborhood where some of the guys on his AAU team played pickup games. Besides Joe, she was the only White person there, but she seemed comfortable. More comfortable even than he was. Joe wasn't used to being in the minority. His school was all White. That doesn't mean everybody was the same, though. Some of the kids, like Marcy and Ed, came from families who had lots of money. Some, like Joe, were from families who had a hard time making it, especially now with the unemployment rate so high. Joe didn't want to go to the pickup games at first, but his mom convinced him that it was good to get out of his comfort zone and try something new.

The orientation activities were kind of boring, but Joe had to admit it was kind of cool to talk with people that he didn't usually hang out with. That's why Joe was a bit surprised at how much he enjoyed the conversations with the other students from his school who were going to the Olympics. Sure it was a little hard to get the conversation started the first few times they got together. Some of the basketball players had bullied Ed during the year, and he especially seemed edgy when Joe went up to him, but by the time they took the school van on the three-hour trip to Washington, D.C., they talked easily together. Ed really cracked Joe up. He knew more than the teachers who were chaperoning, and he wasn't afraid to let them know it. And Marcy, even though she played classical music, loved to listen to Lupe Fiasco, Joe's favorite rapper. Joe even started to appreciate manga a bit, and he promised himself that he'd go to the plays next year.

Figure 4.4

"NEW FRIENDS" TEXT (Continued)

Once Joe arrived at the Olympics, he had to say good-bye to his new school friends. Each kid went off to a different dorm at the college where they were staying. Joe and all the athletes were in a dorm set off from everyone else behind a small wood. Some of the other kids were in apartment style rooms that held eight people. But Joe's dorm only had doubles.

The athletes were an amazing collection of people. His roommate Aban was a soccer player from Iraq. Joe thought that maybe they put an Iraqi kid and an American kid in the same room on purpose, just to show that sports was a way to bring people together. It was pretty interesting to room with Aban. Aban was Muslim. He prayed five times every day. And he had lots of amazing stories to tell about the war. Sometimes American soldiers were the heroes. But sometime they were the villains. Aban didn't seem to hold that against Joe, though Aban tended to hang out with the other Muslim kids. But after a few days, they were comfortable with each other, and they started to share their hopes and dreams in quiet whispers after lights out in the dorm. It didn't seem so odd to be talking with someone so different. Everyone at the camp was doing it.

But Joe did have a chance to hang out with basketball players too. He and this Nigerian kid Chinedu had great one-on-one games. The both played small forward. Both were already 6'2" and were still growing. Both liked to drive to the basket but could use more practice on their outside shot. After their games, they'd talk. Joe found out that Chinedu's family was really rich because his dad was in the oil business. His life was so different from Joe's on that end. Joe had never even gone to the movies because his mom couldn't afford it. Sometimes at dinner he and Sharon would talk about how unfair it seemed that some of the kids they were meeting had so much when the two of them had single moms who had to struggle.

And then there was the dorm counselor, Enrique, a 45-year-old teacher from Venezuela. Joe had never met anyone like him. And he didn't know much about Venezuela except something that his social studies teacher had said about the fact that Venezuela had a president who hated the United States. Enrique didn't know a thing about sports, at least not about basketball. But he sure was willing to learn. Joe had never met an adult who listened so hard to kids. Enrique mostly listened, but when he talked it was really worth paying attention to. He seemed so wise about so many things: friends, girls, school, you name it. Most nights everyone would gather around Enrique, talking about anything and everything, from what happened on the courts or fields to what was happening at home.

Joe was really sorry when the three weeks were over. The whole experience was a life-changing one. The last days there everyone exchanged e-mail addresses and promised to add each other as Myspace friends.

Source: Smith and Wilhelm (2010).

Available for download from **www.corwin.com/uncommoncore**.

"NEW FRIENDS" ACTIVITY

NAME: _____ DATE: _____

Think about Joe and all the people he has met. Rank them from the person Joe is most likely to stay friends with (1), to the person Joe is least likely to stay friends with (7). Be prepared to defend your answers.

_____ Marcy, the cellist

_____ Sharon, the actress

_____ Ed, the braniac

_____ Zack, the manga artist

_____ Aban, the roommate

_____ Chinedu, the basketball player

_____ Enrique, the dorm counselor

Which of the following had the greatest influence of your rankings? Please give a 1 to the factor that was most influential down to a 5 for the one that was least influential.

_____ The way things were at Joe's school

_____ The way things tend to be in middle schools in general

_____ The economic situation and issues of social class and status

_____ The kind of person Joe's mom was at home

_____ The kind of place the camp was

_____ How other countries thought of the United States

Figure 4.5

3. Develop Robust Problems That Foster Engagement While Requiring Attention to the Text

The series of questions in David Coleman's model lessons on the "Gettysburg Address" suggest that the majority of the questions a teacher should ask about a text are ones focused on particular details of particular parts of the text. Although the model lessons do not provide authentic questions that call upon students to employ the understandings they gained from their close reading (e.g., What do you make of the fact that Lincoln did not explicitly mention slavery?), Coleman's discussions of text-dependent questions suggests that he would approve of such questions as long as they came after a close reading.

Our worry about the domination of such narrowly focused questions is that they will have negative effects on students. First, there's the issue of pacing. Three days on the "Gettysburg Address" is an awfully long time. Second, there's the issue of sameness. Tackling one text after another in the same methodological manner certainly runs the risk of boredom. It promotes a fixed versus a dynamic mind-set toward reading and one's own capacities that undermine the spirit of the CCSS. Finally, we return to what research on classroom discourse clearly establishes: Open discussion of authentic questions leads to higher achievement on complex literacy tasks. Coleman's questions on the "Gettysburg Address" might lead students to Coleman's understanding of the text, but they certainly wouldn't lead to much genuine discussion or to students' transferable capacities to come to their own interpretations.

For all of these reasons, we advocate developing a repertoire for framing readings in the context of problems that require and reward the development of the strategies targeted in the anchor standards. It's beyond the scope of this book to provide an exhaustive list, but below we highlight one idea that appears in Coleman's plans on the "Gettysburg Address" that we think warrants more attention and then add two of our own.

Essential Questions

Given Anchor Standard 6, which requires that students consider how *purpose* shapes a text, and the research that supports inquiry approaches to learning (see, e.g., Wilhelm, 2007), think about this:

Coleman's narrowly focused questions promote a fixed versus a dynamic mind-set toward reading that undermines the spirit of the CCSS.

Process for Coupling Maxi-Lessons on Strategies With Text-Specific Applications of Those Strategies

1. Identify a focal strategy.

2. Engage students in understanding that strategy.

3. Provide lots of practice in applying the strategy to a series of texts.

4. Ask students to apply the strategy to their independent reading.

5. Solicit evidence for conclusions they drew from their application of the strategy.

Box 4.3

How can we pose an essential question for students about the "Gettysburg Address"—or any other text—that provides them with a problem orientation to the reading?

Three possibilities for "Gettysburg Address" immediately occur to us:

- How can we best respond to tragedy?

- How can we best memorialize events and people?

- How can we find the value in horrific events?

(More on these kinds of essential questions in the next chapter.)

If we use an essential question we can proceed to consider how well the text—whatever the text that we are reading might be—addresses the problem summarized in the essential question.

Buried in Appendix II of the Gettysburg Address we discussed earlier is the information that Lincoln wrote five versions of the address (the five versions can be found here: http://www.gettysburgfoundation.org/41). Asking students to read different versions and discuss the possible rationale for and effectiveness of the changes in each could possibly generate open discussion. For example, an earlier version of the address had the sentence "We have come to dedicate a portion of it, as a final resting place for those who died here, that the nation might live" while the final version had this one: "We have come to dedicate a portion of that field, as a final resting place for those who here gave their lives that that the nation might live."

Unfortunately, the "Instructional Commentary" provided for the lesson undercuts the potential power of the activity by indicating that students "should be poised to discuss how changes such as this add solemnity and the notion of sacrifice to the final version." Isn't it at least worth arguing that "gave their lives" sanitizes the horror of the battlefield and so diminishes the sacrifice that the soldiers made? As writers, we're very much aware that all of the changes we make in our writing do not necessarily improve it—that, as Anchor Standards 4 through 6 emphasize, authorial choices lead to different meanings and effects.

Even if you don't have multiple versions of a text, you can create your own different versions (you are meeting Anchor Standard 9 either way). What if the sentence above had been written "We have come to dedicate a portion of that field, as a final resting place for those Union soldiers who here gave their lives that that nation might live." How about "We have come to dedicate a portion of that field, as a final resting place for those who here were killed and maimed so that that nation might live"?

Responding to what version is most effective demands that students understand both the overarching purpose of the address (something the essential question assists with) and the rhetorical means by which it is achieved. It teaches students that texts aren't inevitable—that is, that they are the result of choices made by their creators that are more or less effective in achieving their purpose. But this excellent problem can only work if it's treated as an authentic question, not merely as an indication or illustration of the *teacher's* understanding.

Open discussion of authentic questions leads to higher achievement on complex literacy tasks.

The Most Important Word

We can also generate a problem to grapple with if we ask students this:

> What's the most important word (for a shorter text), or
> section, character, or scene (for a longer text)?

Try it with the "Gettysburg Address." What's the most important word? Deborah thinks it's "unfinished" and would argue that the significance of the "Gettysburg Address" is that it gives notice to the unfinished work of equality that still remains left to complete more than 150 years after the address was delivered. Jeff thinks it's "equal" since it concludes the introduction, which gives it resonance, and because Lincoln had been involved in a process of making the war less about state's rights and more about slavery and equality in order to keep Britain and France out of the war. Michael thinks it's "Liberty." He points to the capitalization and would argue that the word puts the issue of slavery front and center without turning attention away from the battlefield itself.

If you play out the discussion in your mind, you'll see that as it continues, all of us would have to turn back to the text again and again for support. This is the kind of close reading that everyone is talking about. At the same time, it's reminding students that one of their primary jobs as a reader, especially a reader of long texts, is to determine importance.

Semantic Differential Scales

Still another way to approach problem solving is to use semantic differential scales. Semantic differential scales contain pairs of words that are opposites. To use them, simply ask students to place the text somewhere on the scale. For example, in a discussion of the "Gettysburg Address" you could ask students to place the text on any one or all of the six-point scales shown in Figure 4.6.

You can use the same scales throughout a unit or develop new ones for each text under consideration. We suggest having students fill them out individually. Then they work in small groups and discuss. Another option is to tape a scale on the floor in front of your classroom and have them vote with their feet. Once they've chosen their spot we ask them to pick a partner who chose a different scale point and discuss it. Once

SEMANTIC SCALE FOR THE "GETTYSBURG ADDRESS"

NAME: _____ DATE: _____

Optimistic   Pessimistic

Inclusive   Exclusive

Backward   Future
looking   oriented

Figure 4.6

again we invite you to imagine these lively discussions in your mind. We know they require the same attention to the text that text-dependent questions do, particularly if you ask students to justify their answers in ways that include some references to the texts in question.

4. Develop Activities That
Necessitate Metacognitive Understandings

If you buy the argument that teaching for transfer is our most important goal and that cultivating mindfulness is critical for fostering transfer, then it's important to create contexts that require students to articulate the strategies they employ using what Beers and Probst (2013) call "generalizable language" (p. 89). Following are a couple of ways you can do this.

Symbolic Story Representation

One way to encourage students to articulate their strategies is to make regular use of symbolic story representations (for full descriptions of this technique, see Wilhelm, 2007). To do a symbolic story representation students first identify a section in a text that they think is especially important or compelling. Then they represent that scene either realistically or symbolically by making cutouts that represent the characters in the scene, the relationships among the characters, themselves as readers, and, importantly, the strategies they employed while reading it. Finally, they talk through their experience reading the scene, moving the reader cutout—and other cutouts—to tell the story of their reading and to name their developing understandings, changes in how they played the role of the reader, and so on. If you remember Colorforms™ you have a sense of what the students' creations could look like.

The reader cutouts are crucial as they force students to use generalizable and hence transferable language to talk about their reading. Here's a portion of one student's symbolic story representation on *Reach!* by Laila Ali, reconstructed from some of Jeff's field notes:

> So here's my introduction to my [symbolic story representation]. For the reader cutout, I decided I would be a Boxing Glove [holds up a cutout of boxing glove] because I wanted to be part of her and live through her experience but I don't like boxing and can't imagine myself fighting, so I wasn't really able to be her, but I could be with her. A glove fits over part of a person and can be with that person and even protect that person, but it isn't the person, and that kind of summarized how I related to Laila. I try to live through her experience, but I can't always, so I could be taken off or watch things from the side. [Shows us photos of Muhammad Ali and Laila and photos of her dad and herself.] Ali and Leila were really the two major characters, so I used these photos to show them and how I related to them.

This book also made me think a lot about how my relationship with my dad was like that of Laila to her dad. So you'll see how I tuck our photos behind theirs. When their relationship comes up, you'll see how I show how they are relating by moving their photos, but then I make almost like a mirror map of how my dad and I related during a similar situation in our life. My dad isn't famous like Ali, but he's a teacher and so most of the kids like around here know him, so there are some similarities because he is like famous in our town. Now I know it is an autobiography, and so I have to read it in a special way, because I know it is supposed to help me understand her life and that I am supposed to learn [from autobiographies] about people's lives and compare the lessons I learn to my own [life]. I also know that maybe I shouldn't believe everything because she is going to want to present herself in a good way. Now I made a cutout of a stage whenever I felt she was performing her own life or showing me something about how to arrange and perform my own life. And I made these dark glasses [holds them up] when I felt I should be skeptical of something she said. And I made these clear glasses when I felt I was seeing something really clearly, and then I made this magnifying glass [holds it up] when there was something I had to pay attention to and see clearly.

Pretty amazing. But also pretty instructive, both for how the student read *Reach!* and how she (and others) might read autobiographies in the future.

Sharing Understandings

Another possibility is to have students share their understandings about reading with other students. For example, when Michael's methods students worked with seventh and eighth graders in local schools on their reading, the culminating project was creating a *Good Reader Handbook*, a children's book on how to become good readers. Handbooks included advice on how to make prediction, how to make inferences about characters, how to examine multiple perspectives, how to visualize, the kinds of questions readers should ask, how to evaluate the reliability of narrators, and the like.

Our point is this: If we want to make it more likely that students will transfer what they've learned about reading to new reading situations, we have to create occasions in which they have to name what they do. Activities that require them to make their reading visible and hence sharable are a way to do just that.

5. Make Your Reading Visible by Reading Texts With Students for the First Time

We think that it is essential for teachers to make their reading processes—including all their fits and starts, self-monitoring and corrections—visible and available to students. That's why we are a fan of teacher think-alouds and teachers' performing symbolic story representations for their students. Both activities allow teachers to model how they read in ways that students can then borrow.

But sharing works best when you are reading cold, for the first time, with your students. Peter Rabinowitz (Rabinowitz & Smith, 1998) has made an observation that we think is absolutely profound in its simplicity: One of the most salient features of literature classrooms is that teachers are teaching texts that they have read many times to kids who are reading them for the first time. Coleman's emphasis on text-dependent questions that lead students to a teacher's interpretation are likely to make that even more true. He says of the instruction that he advocates, "There's a real shift here. You're spending much more time preparing for instruction by reading carefully yourself and that in fact becomes the main work of preparation" (*Common Core in ELA/Literacy*, 2012).

What's the problem? As Rabinowitz points out, rereading is

> not simply a richer or deeper or more sophisticated reading, but a substantially different kind of activity . . . To put it more fancifully, if reading is a perplexing walk, full of stumbles and confusions and wrong turns, through an unfamiliar forest, [re-reading] is the production of a Park Service map that abstracts from the events of a first reading—transcending the order in which they occurred to show the proper trails. (Rabinowitz & Smith 1998, p. 91)

Look again at the anchor standards of the CCSS. It's pretty clear to us that they call for students to be able to negotiate the unfamiliar forests they encounter. In our last section, we discussed creating contexts that required students to share the way they read. Reading along with our students is a way that teachers can share their own way of reading. The questions teachers ask come only after they have figured things out. Reading with students is a way to focus on just how we do that figuring.

Bill Connolly (Connolly & Smith, 2003) took the risk of doing first-time reading along with his students and found that both he and his students benefited. Here are a couple of excerpts from Bill's teaching journal:

> I like how I felt comfortable not knowing it all and equally comfortable giving my opinion or interpretation. . . .

> I have to say that I feel there was respect for my authority (as teacher) but a number of kids had no qualms about disagreeing with me. . . . I feel good about that type of authority. My kids feel comfortable disagreeing with me.

And here's what one student said: "[It] made him more like 'one of us,' that is, we were not hearing responses from someone who knew the poem like the back of his hand." And another:

> Whatever came to mind, I wrote [in my journal]. There was nothing holding me back. The teacher had not read the poem before, so he was doing the same thing as me—trying to understand it.

As a consequence of the disagreements, both Bill and his students had to be clear about why they thought what they thought. They had to return to the texts under consideration to point out evidence. But citing evidence alone won't be enough. In explaining why that evidence leads to a particular conclusion, one has to articulate the rules of notice and interpretive strategies one employed to recognize something as evidence in the first place.

When Bill did this work, he used the procedure highlighted in Box 4.4.

Sharing works best when you are reading cold, for the first time, with your students.

Procedure for Reading an Unknown Text With Your Students

1. Tell a colleague of the instructional context of your class, and ask the colleague to bring in a short text relevant to that context.

2. Write a free response to the text along with your students.

3. Open the discussion by sharing and responding to those responses, taking care to highlight the generalizable moves that you and your students made.

Box 4.4

6. Develop Instructional Strategies for Fostering High-Level Academic Talk

We're all teacher educators, so we've all spent many, many hours working with our preservice teachers to understand that a list of questions, even the very best questions, is not a lesson plan. We want our preservice teachers to think hard about when to call on volunteers and when to seek a comment from someone whose hand isn't up. We want them to use different kinds of small groups and to place those groups into different kinds of relations with whole-class discussion. We want them to develop routines so that students expect that they'll have to elaborate their answers. We want them to create the expectation for accountable talk by making sure students are listening hard to what their classmates are saying.

A complete examination of classroom discussion could be a book in itself. (For an outstanding example see *Talking in Class: Using Discussion to Enhance Teaching and Learning*; McCann, Johannessen, Kahn, & Flanagan, 2006.) But let's take one moment to examine a few suggestions that emerge from the research.

Nystrand (1997) found that classroom discussions that were associated with larger improvements in performance over the year were characterized by three things:

- Authentic questions
- Time for open discussion among at least three student participants
- Uptake—that is, when a teacher's question builds on a previous student question

We've already discussed authentic questions, so we won't repeat ourselves here. But let's think for a minute about classroom routines that help teachers enact the other two criteria. In whole-class discussions, the floor typically returns to the teacher after each student turn. We work with our preservice students to foster student-to-student interactions by developing ways to orchestrate discussions that allow them to step back. For example, instead of calling on one student, a teacher can call on three or four—you, then you, then you, then

you—requiring students to take at least four consecutive turns. Or teachers can develop a routine in which students call on their classmates.

We also encourage our students to make use of *uptake*, both by asking questions that probe for elaboration (e.g., "Can you tell us more about that?") and by developing orchestrating moves that call for students to examine what their classmates have said (e.g., "OK, Sarah and John seem to disagree here. What do you all think?"). As we said, we don't want to go too far afield here, but we do want to make the point that Coleman's emphasis on *what* questions to ask means that he neglects thinking about *how* to ask those questions.

Moving Students to Independence

Here's what Coleman (2011) says about the instruction he modeled on "Letter From Birmingham Jail":

> I want to be clear about the word "independent" because the standards require independence in the sense kids have to be able do what I did with that letter on their own, meaning without the kind of prompting and questioning [I provided]. They have to gain that independence to be college and career ready. (p. 25)

We couldn't agree more strongly. That's why we're so dismayed by Coleman's emphasis on text-dependent questions, especially in light of the fact that no research of which we're aware demonstrates that such questions result in independence. What research on transfer teaches us is that students must have conscious control over what they will transfer and plenty of practice in doing so. Research on classroom discourse teaches us that the asking of authentic questions that foster open discussion among students, discussions in which they can hear and evaluate multiple interpretations, is associated with improved performance on complex literacy tasks. Once again, Coleman's emphasis on text-dependent questions would seem to be at odds with what we know.

We hope that it's clear that our critique of text-dependent questions is not based on a desire for classroom discussions in which anything goes. We believe that there's an ethical imperative to treat authors and the texts they create respectfully. But we also believe we have an ethical obligation to prepare our students for the future and to act on the best knowledge we have about how to do so. Focusing on particular texts through teacher-generated text-dependent questions doesn't fulfill that obligation. What does is cultivating mindfulness among students by giving them repeated practice applying strategies in contexts that reward their use.

No Text Is an Island 5

How to Get Students Farther With Text-by-Text Sequencing

In our last chapter, we pointed out that David Coleman seems to believe that effective instruction focuses on the teaching of individual texts. One manifestation of that belief is his emphasis on text-dependent questions, an emphasis that we argued is misguided. Another manifestation of that belief is his emphasis on teaching texts in isolation from one another. Our worry about this emphasis, one that's demonstrated by some of the Standards themselves, is that it runs counter both to what we know about how people read and develop their reading abilities and to what we know about effective curricular organization. Our purpose in this chapter is to explain our worries and to suggest ways to put texts into meaningful conversation with each other in order to help students do the rigorous work the Standards require.

Where the Authors of the Standards Go Wrong About Text-to-Text Connections

As we discussed in Chapter 2, schema theory explains how learning proceeds by connecting the *known* to the *new*. You can think of schema as bookshelves in your brain, structures on which you can store information. You might remember the examples we discussed in Chapter 2 to illustrate the notion of schema. Here's another one from a classic study by Bransford and Johnson (1972):

> The procedure is actually quite simple. First you arrange things into different groups. Of course, one pile may be sufficient depending on how much there is to do. If you have to go somewhere else due to lack of facilities that is the next step, otherwise you are pretty well set. It is important not to overdo things. That is, it is better to do too few things at once than too many. In the short run this may not seem important but complications can easily arise. A mistake can be expensive as well. At first the whole procedure will seem complicated. Soon, however, it will become just another facet of life. It is difficult to foresee any end to the necessity for this task in the immediate future, but then one never can tell. After the procedure is completed one arranges the materials into different groups again. Then they can be put into their appropriate places. Eventually they will be used once more and the whole cycle will then have to be repeated. However, that is part of life. (p. 722)

How comfortable are you that you understand the passage? Now imagine if you read the title "Doing the Laundry" first." Makes all the difference, doesn't it? And the difference is that the title activates your prior knowledge, providing you with the resources you need to for comprehend the text.

When we read, we relate the content of our reading to what we already know in an act called *assimilation*. If the new and the known don't fit together, then existing schema must be adjusted to accommodate the new learning. Without such accommodation, people will not only fail to understand new information, but they will also quickly revert to prior misconceptions (Science Media Group, 1989; see also Dykstra, 2006; Wieman, 2005).

But knowledge of content is not all that readers need. They also need knowledge of genre. By genre we don't mean the very, very broad groupings (short story, poem, and so on) that characterize discussion of genre in school literature anthologies. Rather, what we call genres are groups of texts that, in the words of Wayne Booth (1974), locate readers in a "fairly narrow groove" (p. 99). That is, genres as we understand them put very similar kinds of demands on readers. Rabinowitz (1993) explains: "Genres can . . . be seen not only formally, as sets of features, but from the reader's perspective, as packages of interpretive procedures for unlocking literary secrets through a process of transformation" (p. 334). A couple of quick examples: When we read mysteries, we know there are going to be red herrings, suspects who are introduced to divert our attention from who really did it. When we read a Petrarchan sonnet, we know that the eight-line octave is followed by a six-line sestet and we know that our job as a reader is to put the two parts of the sonnet into meaningful relation.

But, of course, not all genres are literary. The following example will illustrate that Rabinowitz's ideas are relevant beyond literature. Let's take another look at the comics. Some strips are serials that include recurring characters. The authors of those strips expect readers to recognize and at least provisionally care about the characters. *Baldo* is one example. It chronicles the life of Latino teen as he, in the words of a blurb from Amazon.com, balances "his mainstream sensibilities with his Latino heritage."

Other strips work in different ways. Some—we'll call them joke-a-day strips—may not have recurring characters, or if they do, use those characters only as vehicles for a joke, much as one might use an absent-minded professor or other stock character. One such strip is *Pearls Before Swine*. Here's a description drawn from Amazon.com's advertising a recent collection of that strip:

> In this third collection of the immensely popular *Pearls Before Swine*, Stephan Pastis again takes us into the world of Rat, Pig, Zebra, and Goat, and he shows once more just how outrageous—and how hilarious—the unpredictable can be.

Let's look at how readers responded to a recent example of each strip. Here are readers of *Baldo* responding to Baldo's announcement that he likes that school is starting because has a new girlfriend this year:

- Cruz [Baldo's best friend] begs to differ. (Is Rayna, the girl in the computer screen on wheels, just a friend who happens to be a girl to him?)

- Cruz doesn't seem pleased for some reason.

- Maybe Cruz realizes that this is the beginning of the end of their BFFdom. Happened to me. Girls can really mess with your head.

- Way to go, Baldo!!

And here are responses to a recent *Pearls Before Swine*:

- gotta love Pastis' lame puns

- That joke almost hurt physically.

- goat's wrong . . . pastis radiates punniness!

- Puhleeze . . . no more punishment like that, Stephan!

> Readers must apply both their prior *conceptual* knowledge and their knowledge of the strategies required by specific *genres* to successfully navigate texts.

The responses strongly suggest that readers of the strips clearly understand that the strips work in different ways and that the authors of the strips are expecting something different from them. Readers understand that Pastis's strip does not invite them to care about Rat the way readers care about Baldo. Instead, they realize that they have to be ready to recognize and appreciate his wordplay and satire. We could go on spinning out the theory that we're introducing here (see Rabinowitz & Smith, 1998, for a book-length treatment), but suffice it to say that we hope we've established that readers put the texts that they read on a mental grid and that that grid has at least two dimensions: the conceptual and the generic/strategic. That is, readers must apply both their prior *conceptual* knowledge and their knowledge of the stances and strategies required by specific *genres* to successfully navigate texts. Unfortunately, the Common Core State Standards (CCSS) themselves don't seem to recognize fully the import of these fundamental moves that successful readers must make.

"Wait a minute" you might say. "The reading Standards for each grade include a section called 'Integration of Knowledge and Ideas.' It's unfair to say Coleman and the other authors of the Standards document argue for the teaching of individual texts as discrete and autonomous events." Let's take a look at those Standards and see how they hold up. For the sake of brevity, we'll just look at the Standards from every other grade level.

The sixth-grade Standards in the Integration of Knowledge and Ideas domain include the following:

> **CCSS.ELA-Literacy.RL.6.7.** Compare and contrast the experience of reading a story, drama, or poem to listening to or viewing an audio, video, or live version of the text, including contrasting what they "see" and "hear" when reading the text to what they perceive when they listen or watch.

> (**RL.6.8** not applicable to literature)

> **CCSS.ELA-Literacy.RL.6.9.** Compare and contrast texts in different forms or genres (e.g., stories and poems; historical novels and fantasy stories) in terms of their approaches to similar themes and topics.

In Standard 6.7 the focus is on examining multiple versions of the same text. However, Standard 6.9 would seem to suggest some kind of thematic grouping. But as we'll see, subsequent Standards for grade 8 don't echo that call for connecting texts:

> **CCSS.ELA-Literacy.RL.8.7.** Analyze the extent to which a filmed or live production of a story or drama stays faithful to or departs from the text or script, evaluating the choices made by the director or actors.

> (**RL.8.8** not applicable to literature)

> **CCSS.ELA-Literacy.RL.8.9.** Analyze how a modern work of fiction draws on themes, patterns of events, or character types from myths, traditional stories, or religious works such as the Bible, including describing how the material is rendered new.

Both eighth-grade Standards in the Integration of Knowledge and Ideas domain seem to us to focus primarily on integrating knowledge to increase one's understanding of a central text. In 8.7, the analysis focuses on faithfulness to the text, which means the emphasis is on the original text rather than on any kind of conversation *across* texts. In 8.9, understanding a source text provides a resource for understanding the more modern text.

The grades 11–12 Standards in the Integration of Knowledge and Ideas domain are as follows:

> **CCSS.ELA-Literacy.RI.11–12.7.** Integrate and evaluate multiple sources of information presented in different media or formats (e.g., visually, quantitatively) as well as in words in order to address a question or solve a problem.

> **CCSS.ELA-Literacy.RI.11–12.8.** Delineate and evaluate the reasoning in seminal U.S. texts, including the application of constitutional principles and use of legal reasoning (e.g., in U.S. Supreme Court majority opinions and dissents) and the premises, purposes, and arguments in works of public advocacy (e.g., *The Federalist*, presidential addresses).

> **CCSS.ELA-Literacy.RI.11–12.9.** Analyze seventeenth-, eighteenth-, and nineteenth-century foundational U.S. documents of historical and literary significance (including The Declaration of Independence, the Preamble to the Constitution, the Bill of Rights, and Lincoln's Second Inaugural Address) for their themes, purposes, and rhetorical features.

Standard 11–12.7 seems to us to be a writing standard and not a reading standard. Standards 11–12.8 and 11–12.9 strikingly call for the analysis of individual texts and make no mention of developing knowledge across a series of texts. So of the seven specific Standards in the Integration of Knowledge and Ideas domain that we've examined, only one calls for grouping multiple texts together as a way to develop knowledge *across* texts. Moreover, while the CCSS document includes a table titled "Staying on Topic Within a Grade and Across Grades: How to Build Knowledge Systematically in English Language Arts K–5," no such table appears for grades 6 through 12.

The Standards' tendency to focus on teaching individual texts in isolation is exacerbated by the writing and speaking David Coleman and his colleagues have done in support of the Standards. In the *Revised Publishers' Criteria for the Common Core State Standards in English Language Arts and Literacy, Grades 3–12,* Coleman and Pimentel (2012) discuss what they term key criteria for text selection at great length. They focus primarily on two criteria: (1) complexity and (2) range and quality. Here are the only two references in those criteria to reading different materials and putting them into conversation with each other to stimulate thinking and understanding:

> Aligned materials for grades 3–12 should set out a coherent selection and sequence of texts (of sufficient complexity and quality) to give students a well-developed sense of bodies of literature (like American literature or classic myths and stories) as part of becoming college and career ready.

> ***Within a sequence or collection of texts, specific anchor texts are selected for especially careful reading.*** Often in research and other contexts, several texts will be read to explore a topic. It is essential that such materials include a selected text or set of texts that can act as cornerstone or anchor text(s) that make careful study worthwhile. The anchor text(s) provide essential opportunities for students to spend the time and care required for close reading and to demonstrate in-depth comprehension of a specific source or sources. (p. 6)

The guidelines make no mention of principles of sequencing that would help students develop knowledge text by text and to make the kind of intertextual connections experienced readers make as a matter of course. In fact, the writing about "cornerstone" texts suggests a worry that reading across texts would somehow compromise "in-depth comprehension of a single source."

We see that worry reflected in Coleman and his colleague's treatment of the "Gettysburg Address" (Achieve the Core, 2013). In the first place, it's described as a "unit." But instruction related to single text can't be a unit, at least as we understand units. Cunningham (2009) explains that "unit plans consist of concepts and learning goals that are taught over a period of time and are woven together." That weaving seems to us to be the *sine qua non* of units, and we see none of it in Coleman and his colleagues' example. In fact, it seems as though they actively resist making some intertextual connections that are readily available. Here's their commentary about one question they suggest asking about the first paragraph: "What important thing happened in 1776?"

> This question, of course, goes beyond the text to explore students' prior knowledge and associations. Students may or may not know that the Declaration of Independence was issued in 1776, but they will likely know it is a very important date—one that they themselves have heard before. *Something very important happened on that date.* It's OK to mention the Declaration, but the next step is to discover what students can infer about 1776 from Lincoln's own words now in front of them. (Achieve the Core, 2013)

It's okay to mention the "Declaration." But why wouldn't a teacher want to require the reading of it as part of the lesson? Is it even conceivable that anyone in Lincoln's intended audience wouldn't bring knowledge of the "Declaration" to his or her attempt to understand and respond to the "Address"? Whether you agree with the pedagogical suggestion or not, it seems pretty clear that what's important to Coleman and his colleagues is "Lincoln's own words now in front of them" not the intertextual grid against which experienced readers and listeners would place those words in order to engage with them.

Why It Matters

We worry that the emphasis in the CCSS and in Coleman's writing on teaching texts in isolation will exacerbate a tendency in our profession to ignore the power of sequencing. In Michael's school, teachers raced to the bookroom to sign up for which of the required books they wanted to teach first, something he never understood. If the *Odyssey* is the right book to teach first in a ninth-grade course, shouldn't everyone be teaching it then? Jeff never understood why he had to teach *To Kill a Mockingbird* before *Romeo and Juliet* or how that sequence helped students develop knowledge or learn something in one unit that they could use and build on in the next. Deborah's high school curriculum paid little attention to sequencing, so she sought to develop smaller intertextual links, for example, by beginning her teaching of Steinbeck's *Of Mice and Men*, with Robert Burns's poem "To a Mouse." Texts do speak to each other (sometimes explicitly), and one important skill that we want good readers to develop is to understand and make use of those intertextual relationships.

In fact, the reading behaviors of experienced readers often reflect the importance of making intertextual links. In writing this book, we read lots and lots about the CCSS, and our understanding of and response to each text was informed by our reading all the others. In our pleasure reading, we tend to select authors, genres, and themes that are our special favorites. Part of the pleasure we derive from that reading is the depth of understanding that such targeted reading allows. The potential for greater engagement and motivation is there too. Adult readers often go on a thematic tear after becoming interested a place, time, or idea and want to extend that knowledge by reading related books.

What we've found in our own experience is borne out by research. When Applebee, Burroughs, and Stevens (2000) examined the curricular structure of the classes of a group of experienced and highly regarded literature teachers, they found that in the vast majority of them, teachers and students made very few connections across texts. Anagnostopoulos's (2000) study, which focused on urban schools, came to a similar conclusion. She found that the connections among activities in a given class period and over several days were tenuous at best. Examinations of teachers' curricular plans indicated that events were sequenced with no necessary connections among them. For example, one day's work in class might include a vocabulary drill, feedback on compositions returned, and the reading of a text followed by a brief discussion, with no connection of the text to the vocabulary or the writing.

> We worry that the emphasis in the CCSS and in Coleman's writing on teaching texts in isolation will exacerbate our tendency to ignore the power of sequencing.

Examination of teachers' curricular plans for the year revealed that they were similarly disjointed, a mere list of terms and works to be "covered." For example, one teacher intended to teach the elements of literature: plot, character, mood, theme, and so forth. She expected to teach these in reference to a list of short stories. The novel would be taught in reference to *The Pearl*, which means that the teacher planned to teach the content of that novel as revealed in the contents of her quizzes and tests. Students would be required to supply short definitions of the forms (e.g., short story and novel) and elements of literature, and to recall information from their reading. In practice, however, when students could not pass these tests and quizzes, teachers frequently provided points for unrelated activities. For example, teachers sometimes gave extra points for coming to class on time or for bringing books to class.

The result of this sort of planning is that the cognitive structures on which students focus are low-level ones, low level because they have few connections to other ideas. That is, once students have learned the simple definition of plot required by the teacher (e.g., "what happens in a story"), there is nowhere to go with it. Plot, as it was taught by the teachers in Anagnostopoulos's study, was simply not a generative concept that students could apply to their subsequent reading. She found that the focus of the curriculum is on bits and pieces of information. Students did not learn concepts that they were able to apply productively to future tasks.

Our colleagues in math and science think hard about sequence, recognizing that Chapter 1 prepares students for Chapter 2, which prepares students for Chapter 3, and so on. They recognize that certain concepts and procedures are prerequisite to mastering more complex ones. Shouldn't we do the same? Not according to the CCSS and its authors, at least as evidenced by their lack of attention to principles of sequence in the CCSS document.

But if we did, good things would follow. Turning again to Applebee and his colleagues (2000), when curricula were integrated, "the benefits of such curricula seemed real . . . in terms of the depth of discussion they provoked and the enthusiasm exhibited by both teachers and students" (p. 425).

So what to do? How do we help our students achieve the kind of reading and interpretive skills we and the authors of the Standards want them to without sacrificing the integrity and coherence of a language arts curriculum? We have three suggestions.

How You Can Get It Right: Three Strategies for Developing Knowledge Across Texts

1. Develop Carefully Sequenced Units That Develop Knowledge Text by Text

We've argued extensively elsewhere (Smith & Wilhelm, 2002, 2006, 2010; Wilhelm, 2007; Wilhelm & Novak, 2011) about the power of developing units built around essential questions (EQs). EQs, as we understand them, are the deep and abiding questions we all face as we think about our lives:

- What makes a hero?
- Does an individual's success depend more on the individual or the environment?
- What keeps us together and what pulls us apart?

Reading matters when it gives readers insight into questions like these. And as a consequence, instruction built around EQs fosters the kind of *deep talk* (Appleman, 2006) that counters objections to English so chillingly articulated by one teenager in Michael and Jeff's (Smith & Wilhelm, 2006) study of the literate lives of boys both in and out of school:

> English is about NOTHING! It doesn't help you DO anything.
> English is about reading poems and telling about rhythm. It's
> about commas and crap like that for God's sake. What does that
> have to DO with DOING anything? It's about NOTHING! (p. 25)

But the benefits of units built around EQs extend beyond the motivation that the content and its clear connection to students' lives provide. The units are also motivating because students spend lots of time exploring an issue and in doing so develop the background knowledge that makes subsequent reading more accessible. Think about your own reading life. If you're like us, most of the reading you do is designed to deepen existing areas of expertise rather than to develop new ones. Why? It's hard to read in a new domain until you know enough to be comfortable there.

But rather than share our arguments, let's share the experience of a group of elementary school teachers from the Boise State Writing Project who worked together to design instruction for the wide range of students that they taught.

A Unit on Friendship

The group first solicited their own fourth-grade students to see what was most compelling to them. Friendship and bullying came out as major topics across the different groups of students. So the teachers framed their units around the essential question:

What is a true friend?

They included several subquestions such as this one:

How can we encourage ourselves and others to be better friends?

Notice that the group did not start with a text; they started with their students and what mattered most to them and their interactions with the world right now as well as in the future.

The group then developed activities and found readings of various kinds that they thought would be compelling to their students, that would help them explore the essential question, and that would require the development of new strategic competence.

The teachers began the unit with powerful frontloading activities. The first was a simple brainstorm about the top 10 features of a good friend and then a survey. The next activity involved ranking actions on the basis of how much true friendship was shown. The students had to provide explanations for their rankings. These activities are provided in Figures 5.1 and 5.2.

BEING A TRUE FRIEND

NAME: _____ DATE: _____

What do you think are the 10 most important qualities of a true friend? List your top 10 in order of importance from 1 (most important) to 10 (least important) athlete. As a class, we will tally the results of our top friendship qualities

Answer the following "would you" questions about friendship. Yes, No, or Maybe.

_____ 1. Would you loan your friend $100?

_____ 2. Would you tell your friend your deepest secret?

_____ 3. Would you lie to your friend to protect his or her feelings?

_____ 4. Would you end your relationship with your friend if she or he did something purposefully hurtful to you?

_____ 5. Would you willing to "take the rap" for something your friend did?

_____ 6. Would you let your friend cheat off your homework or test paper?

_____ 7. Would you miss an important trip or game if your friend needed you?

_____ 8. Would you hide your friend if she or he was wanted by police?

_____ 9. Would you be willing to risk death for your friend?

_____ 10. Would you talk behind your friend's back if his or her new haircut was terrible?

In your small groups, debate your answers. What are the conditions under which you would do or not do the things in the "would you" questions?

_____

_____

_____

_____

_____

Figure 5.1

ACTS OF FRIENDSHIP

NAME: _____ DATE: _____

Rank the following acts of friendship from the one that best shows true friendship (1) to the one that shows the least true friendship.

_____ Turn a friend in to the police for using drugs (or doing something else personally harmful, like a video game addiction)

_____ Tell a guidance counselor that your friend is using drugs

_____ Take a friend to drug counseling and go with them

_____ Tell your friend you won't do drugs with them, but their business is their business

_____ Do drugs with your friend out of friendship and camaraderie

_____ Say you don't want to see them or be around them as long as they are hurting themselves

_____ Take a friend in after being kicked out of his or her house

_____ Make the friend go back home and try to reach an understanding with his or her parents

_____ Give your friend some money to get started on his or her own

_____ Go with your friend to his or her house and support him or her in conversing with the parents

_____ Go with your friend to a homeless shelter to get him or her settled there

With your learning group, come up with other things one might do to demonstrate true friendship and place them among the ones in the list.

_____

_____

_____

_____

_____

Figure 5.2

Students then examined and wrote more elaborated scenarios (see Figure 5.3 for the assignment given students) and shared them, thereby becoming authors of complex texts that others would read and put into conversation with still other texts to create conversation and a web of meaning. The students then rewrote their scenarios to have different endings. The writing provided a perfect occasion for addressing a complex interpretive strategy: determining the narrator's relationship with the audience. Lanser (1981) discusses how different narrators take different attitudes toward their audience, ranging from respect to contempt, and that our response to a text is formed in part by our recognizing where we are placed on that continuum and how we feel about it. What's true for stories is true for magazine articles, ads, and orations, so throughout the unit, students can consider how they are being positioned by the author or narrator and what impact that positioning had on their experience of the text. They can also consider how they positioned their readers when they wrote, thereby reading like writers and writing like readers.

Next, students read a story from *Chicken Soup for the Child's Soul* titled "The Forgotten Friend" about a girl who forgets to invite another girl to her birthday party. The students then rewrote the story so the forgotten friend would be included and dramatized their endings through a forum drama technique (see Wilhelm, 2002), comparing each ending in terms of meaning and effect to the ending in the original story in the book. Again, they discussed how an author's creation or sequencing of different events, descriptions, and endings positioned them as readers and how this resulted in meaning and effect.

Students then wrote their own stories of exclusion and rewrote the endings to these. Excellent small- and large-group discussions ensued about what we could learn about friendship from such stories. Next, they were asked to find readings

FRIENDSHIP SCENARIO

You are an athlete and you hang out with other athletes, all of them real straight shooters. Mostly, you spend your free time playing sports, and you always play hoops at recess. There is a really smart, funny girl at school who is in a wheelchair. She is really artistic and a bit loud and crazy. She approaches you and says she wants to be friends and to eat lunch together and hang out some.

How would you react?

How is this being a true friend to your existing friends? To the girl in the wheelchair?

Come up with some problematic scenarios of your own (e.g., what to do when a friend asks you how you like her grotesque new haircut or clothes.) We will brainstorm several ideas as a class and will discuss how to make sure your scenario is problematic and tests out various notions of friendship.

_____

_____

_____

_____

_____

_____

_____

_____

_____

_____

Figure 5.3

about friendship they thought the class would enjoy. Lists and files of readings were compiled by the students, sometimes to be read in literature circle groups and sometimes independently.

The unit continued with students' reading informational texts on friendship, psychological data about friendship, poems, fables, and short stories about friendship. One of the favorite readings was the short story "The Fan Club," which the students engaged in as a story drama (described in full in Wilhelm, 2012b). Eventually, the students read either *Number the Stars* or *Maniac Magee*, two Newberry Award-winning young adult novels that have much to do with friendship on many levels.

Throughout this unit, which lasted nine weeks for most of the teachers, the students kept a huge concept map to help them define "true friend" by citing examples of friendship that came up in readings and discussion as well as their lived experience, counterexamples, general principles of friendship, and a working definition of friendship.

At the end of the unit, all students wrote two different papers:

1. An extended definition of friendship, or of a particular kind of friend, with examples, counterexamples, and so on, using the concept map as a reminder and resource
2. An argument of judgment about what a true friend would do in response to the problematic scenario they developed in response to Activity 3

The students in each class created a "Real Friend Peer Revision Guide" (see Figure 5.4 for the assignment given to students) to guide peer revision in pairs and groups. They tied their work to what had been learned about friendship, and students read each other's work and responded using the guides. Next, students debated their arguments and afterward revised their writing to respond to reservations and complications that arose as a result of the sharing and debate.

Throughout and after the unit, students engaged in various forms of service learning that came up quite naturally and were often suggested by the students themselves:

REAL FRIEND PEER REVISION GUIDE

NAME: _____ DATE: _____

Ask your partner if you have permission to help them.

Ask your partner what kind of help they want—what they want feedback about and what kind and form of feedback works best for them.

First, tell your partner at least one really good thing you want them to KEEP in their paper, and tell them why.

Now, make sure you give really good advice that will help them, and consider their requests of how to help and what to help with.

Provide your partner with at least five more pieces of advice from the following menu.

I wonder what would happen if YOU MOVED . . .

I wonder what would happen if YOU ADDED . . .

I wonder what would happen if YOU DELETED . . .

I wonder what would happen if YOU CHANGED . . .

Remember to phrase your advice in such a way that you are offering friendly, supportive, and helpful advice and that shows you know that your partner is the BOSS of his or her own writing!

Figure 5.4

- **Class Grandparent Project**—Including a class grandparent in class activities—for example, interviewing the grandparent about friendship in different phases of life and providing service to the grandparent such as preparing meals, doing a yard cleanup day, or the like.

- **New Student Mentorship Project**—Mentoring new students to the school, particularly refugee students. This led to a bike project (finding and repairing bikes for refugee students to ride since they did not have transportation) and the creation of a free soccer league (so refugee students could meet others and play soccer since they could not afford the fees for league soccer).

- **New Student/Refugee Parent Project**—Engaging in collaborative writing of school guides for parents in 30 different languages; parent nights; parent–student nights.

- **Friendship Murals**—Creating and posting murals in the schools.

- **Peer Mediation**—Setting up a peer mediation group that worked with students throughout the school for the rest of the year.

Consider these comments by some fourth-grade students on their reflective exit tickets at the end of the unit:

- "I have stood up for people and invited people to play with us. That is the effect that *Maniac Magee* has had on me."

- *"Number the Stars* made me feel closer to people who are different from me because of religion or customs or looks or even the time period they lived in. Like I look at older people differently now, as people too, who lived through stuff."

- "Anne-Marie was risking her life to help others. It made me think that if she could do that then I can help my family and classmates with little things like chores and homework."

At the end of the unit, the teachers agreed that they had met all 32 of the CCSS anchor standards.

Wow. At the end of the unit, the teachers agreed that they had met all 32 of the CCSS anchor standards. What allowed them to do so? The extended engagement in a single conceptual domain that provided the preparation students needed for doing the kind of sophisticated thinking the CCSS call for. One text and activity built toward the next, so students developed ever-deepening strategic facility and conceptual understanding. Had the teachers decided that one of their goals was to have students read Farley's *The Black Stallion*, one of the books selected as a text complexity exemplar for the grade 4–5 band, the unit would certainly have also paved the way for a meaningful engagement with

SIX PRIMARY WAYS TO DEVELOP ESSENTIAL QUESTIONS

1. **Build EQs for your class around issues that your students are working on in other classes**. Say students are the studying American history. You could build a unit around a question like these: How should we judge uses of power? What does it mean to be an American?

2. **Pay attention to the issues** that seem to have the most play in public discourse or that create the most energy in our private discourse, keeping in mind the age of your students and the development appropriateness of each. Michael and his wife Karen are caring for their six-year-old granddaughter. So they are having a second crack at parenting. As a consequence, they've spent countless hours talking about this EQ: What makes a good parent? Deborah's work with the incarcerated has caused her to raise the following EQs: What is justice? What role should considerations of human dignity play in our correctional system? Jeff is passionate about the environment and is constantly asking himself and his friends this question: What is our proper relationship to the natural world? Our increased focus on standardized testing as a measure of student success could also cause us to consider the following EQ: What is the knowledge most worth having? As we are writing this chapter, the nation is embroiled in a debate about what the nation should do in response to finding out that Syria used poison gas on its citizens. That debate centers on this EQ: What are a country's (or person's) obligations to others? If a question can sustain conversation in our lives, it can certainly also do so in our classrooms.

Box 5.1

that text, as it centers on a boy's friendship with a horse and a retired horse trainer.

Guides to Using Essential Questions

Of course, there are limitless other examples of EQs that would be generative. We've developed EQs, as these teachers did, by tapping into students' interests and concerns. This is an excellent way to ensure early buy-in and engagement. In addition to that, we have developed EQs in six primary ways that we can recommend here (see Box 5.1).

3. **Think hard about what makes a text worth teaching.** For example, *Of Mice and Men* raises a number of interesting questions. Two that engage us are these: To what extent is the American Dream equally available to all? Has its availability changed over time?

4. **Examine the assumptions of the CCSS or your state standards** and reframe those assumptions as a question. For example, the introduction to the grade 6–12 reading standards includes this sentence: "Students [who meet the standards] actively seek to understand other perspectives and cultures through reading and listening, and they are able to communicate effectively with people of varied backgrounds." This standard presumes an answer to a question that we think is far from settled: To what extent can people understand each other across demographic (racial, class-based, ethnic, generational, and religious) differences?

5. **Pay attention to your own reading to see what questions attract your interest**. Michael finds himself drawn to new stories about everyday heroes, stories that raise this question: To what extent can one person make a difference in the world? Deborah likes to read contemporary fiction and finds herself wondering about this question: To what extent can children retain their innocence in such a complex world?

6. **Survey your students** to identify issues they've been thinking about.

Once you have an essential question, there are some things to remember when teaching a unit with an EQ at its center (see Box 5.2).

THINGS TO THINK ABOUT WHEN TEACHING UNITS WITH ESSENTIAL QUESTIONS

- **The essential characteristic of essential questions is that they're debatable**, but genuinely debatable questions are very rare in schools. Introduce your unit with an activity that demonstrates the disagreement that exists around a question.

- **If students are responding to debatable questions, then they'll have to make a case** to persuade those who don't share their views. Help them to do so by probing for evidence (e.g., What makes you say so?) and for explanations of how the evidence relates to and supports the claim (e.g., So what?)

- **Units built around EQs put texts in conversation with each other**. So make it a routine to ask questions like these: Of the authors we've read, who would most strongly agree with this author? Who would most strongly disagree? Or return to your frontloading surveys and rankings and ask how authors or characters from different texts would respond.

- **Put literary and nonliterary texts into conversation**.

- **Select a focal reading skill** called for in the CCSS that the texts you choose invite readers to apply.

- **Give students the chance to engage in academic writing and in some other kind of meaningful making**.

Box 5.2

Figure 5.5 presents a planning sheet that we've found useful in creating the kind of units we're suggesting.

Planning Your Own Unit

Let's quickly walk through the kind of thinking you might do with another unit. Say that you teach eighth grade and your colleagues in science begin their course with a unit on heredity. One great way to make connections across disciplines would be to develop a unit around this EQ:

What makes me who I am?

ESSENTIAL QUESTION PLANNING SHEET

NAME: _____ DATE: _____

Essential Question:

Literary Texts	Other Texts	Writing	Other Meaningful Making	Focal Reading Skill	Focal Writing Skill

Figure 5.5

In order to develop the unit and lessons, you'd want to think about the range of possible answers one might give. The nature/nurture debate would surely be relevant and could be covered in science as well as English language arts (ELA). Some would say gender, also applicable in science and ELA. Others might say the time and or place in which one lives. Others would focus on families or the larger culture. Both of these can be explored in social studies classes and ELA. If you want to make it clear to students that there are a variety of answers to the question, then you'll want to have all of these answers represented in some way or another. Working with other teachers can help this to happen.

Backward Planning. Now let's do some backward planning. What would you want your students to write and *make* in the unit? A memoir assignment would seem to flow directly from the question, Who Am I? A collage would help students declare what their provisional answers to the question might be and would fit the Core Standards for multimodal composing. If students are to be able to do a thoughtful job selecting what to include in their memoirs or collages, though, they'll have to at least consider the range of potential responses we've detailed. So what reading would they have to do to evaluate those responses? Studies of identical twins separated at birth would help students engage the nature/nurture debate. Depending on your students, you could read the studies themselves, commentaries on the studies, popular press accounts, or memoirs like *Identical Strangers*, a book about identical twin sisters who were separated at birth and who met for the first time in their mid-30s. Current brain science and the area of neuroplasticity has a lot to say about the nature/nurture debate. There are plenty of popular cultural treatments that could be excerpted, including *The Brain That Changes Itself* by neuroscientist Norman Doidge (2007). Education.com has a page on gender differences (http://www.education.com/topic/gender-differences/) with lots of links.

Of course, literary texts also would help students think seriously about the question. Sandra Cisneros's memoir "Only Daughter" takes up the question of whether being an only daughter "explains everything" about her or whether her Mexican heritage and working-class roots also have explanatory power.

Cisneros's memoir would encourage students to think about gender, class, and ethnicity as influences. Langston Hughes's "Theme for English B" would add race to the conversation. In the short story "Two Kinds," Amy Tan takes up the influence of time and place and family. In "The Pale Mare" by Marian Flandrick Bray, the narrator discusses how she feels constrained by tradition and how it affects her passion to become an astronomer. If you wanted to include one of the text complexity exemplars, *Narrative of the Life of Frederick Douglass, an American Slave* would be a good choice as it would engage students in thinking about the impact of race, geography, time, education, and individual gifts.

Of course, we could go on and on. Instead, let's review. To plan a unit around an essential question, you could employ a process something like the steps laid out in Box 5.3.

Planning a Unit Around an Essential Question

1. Devise an essential question using one of the six techniques discussed above.

2. Consider: What variety of answers could be provided to that question?

3. Select texts of different sorts that suggest one or more of these competing answers.

4. Determine a project that will allow students to present their answers to the question.

5. Plan backward by identifying focal reading and writing skills and conceptual understandings that students will need to develop by the unit's end.

6. Devise frontloading activities, instruction, and a sequence that will help students develop those skills and understandings.

Box 5.3

Many texts of different sorts from different disciplines and of different levels of complexity take up the EQ in some way or another. We'd argue that systematically building knowledge so that students can have meaningful transactions with those more difficult texts is a good idea. But since the CCSS document does not include a figure titled "How to Build Knowledge Systematically in English Language Arts 6–12," the authors of the CCSS must believe that being systematic is important only in the early grades. They must believe that high school students are already prepared—conceptually and strategically—to read and respond to the complex texts they want them to read. Our experience tells us that for most of our students that just isn't the case.

Other Ways to Build Knowledge Text by Text

Units organized around EQs develop conceptual understandings that both motivate and facilitate subsequent reading in the same conceptual domain. But as we noted earlier in this chapter, the conceptual domain comprises only one dimension of the mental grid upon which experienced readers place the texts they encounter. The second is the genre of a text, genre meaning the "narrow groove" in which a text is located not the overbroad very general groupings used by anthologies. Early in this chapter, we looked at comics to illustrate that different kinds of texts work in different ways. That means that the strategic targets in the standard work differently in different kinds of texts. Let's look at the first reading standard as an example. It begins as follows: "Read closely to determine what the text says explicitly and to make logical inferences from it." Seems like an admirable goal, and for most texts, it is. But it's surely not for texts that have unreliable narrators, for what a narrator explicitly says may very well be different from, even the opposite of what an author means.

As Michael (1991) explained in an earlier work, experienced readers have a variety of hot buttons that alert them to become suspicious of a narrator. They ask questions like the following:

- Is the narrator too self-interested to be reliable?
- Is the narrator sufficiently experienced to be reliable?

> Systematically building knowledge so that students can have meaningful transactions with more difficult texts is a good idea.

- Is the narrator sufficiently knowledgeable to be reliable?

- Is the narrator sufficiently moral to be reliable?

- Is the narrator too emotional to be reliable?

- Are the narrator's actions too inconsistent with his or her words to make him or her reliable?

And if the answer to any of those questions is yes, then experienced readers go through the following process:

1. They check the facts that are under dispute.

2. They apply their knowledge of the world.

3. They reconstruct the meaning.

It sounds easy, but it's not, so it takes practice. The most efficient way to get that practice is to read a series increasingly complex of texts with first-person narrators and to talk about them so that students can practice applying the heuristic and can experience its utility.

Other possibilities exist as well: units built around a single author's work, a literary style, maybe even a location. Our point is simply this: While we most strongly endorse the use of EQs, there are other possibilities for developing knowledge text by text. As a teacher, you just have to ask yourself, Are these texts sufficiently conceptually or structurally similar that reading one prepares a reader to read the next? If the answer is yes, then your unit design is supporting your students' achievement.

The benefit of units like the ones we've described derive from the fact that they create extended textual conversations, and students' engagement in these conversations allows them to develop rich conceptual and strategic understandings. When we've made these points at conferences, we've often been approached by teachers who say something like, "Boy, I wish I had the curricular freedom to create such units. I don't. We have to cover a Shakespeare play every year and six (or four or eight) required novels. I just can't bring other materials in."

We recognize that we have a freedom that some teachers don't, but we want to make two points in response. First, the CCSS mandate virtually

> While we most strongly endorse the use of EQs, there are other possibilities for developing knowledge text by text.

no specific readings. They emphasize strategic understandings. They also emphasize an increasing attention to non-narrative texts. Units built around EQs provide a vehicle to address both emphases. As we argued in Chapter 1, we can use the Standards themselves as a lever for progressive practices. Let's do this for the good of our students and the vitality of our teaching!

But even if those arguments don't carry the day, we believe that teachers can move in the direction of designing units of the sort we have discussed. Guthrie, perhaps the leading voice in the field of reading motivation, introduces a construct we find very compelling: micro choices. Guthrie, Klauda, and Morrison (2012) argue that giving students choice is extremely motivating. They note that because "teachers believe they must cover topics by traveling quickly over broad domains, they tend to believe they have little opportunity to afford choice to learners. Although this obstacle is prohibitive, teachers have many opportunities to provide micro choices" (p. 28). One example would be letting each student choose what story from an anthology he or she would like to read.

We think that the concept of micro choices can be usefully extended to teachers even in the most controlled curricular situation. If a teacher has to teach, say, *Romeo and Juliet,* he or she might tell the class that they will be using the text to think about the EQ, What sustains or interferes with love relationships? Students can be assigned to choose a song, news article, magazine feature, or movie synopsis that addresses that question in some way, and each day a student can be asked to lead a brief discussion on the text he or she has selected. The teacher can join in as well, maybe choosing a poem or story. Then, during the discussion of the play, the teacher might regularly ask, "Have we seen that idea any place else? What have we read recently that takes a different position?" It's not quite the same as developing an entire a unit around an EQ, but it's a move in the right direction.

2. Resist Traditional Organizations

If you pick up a literature anthology, chances are it will make use of one of two organizations: broad genre grouping such as the short story or poetry genre or chronology. Here's the problem: These organizations don't support students' developing the complex understandings required by the CCSS. Applebee and his colleagues (2000) found, in fact, that

> other conversations that echo through many high school and
> college literature courses have lost much of the life they once
> had, at least in the ways they were reflected in classrooms
> in the present study. Questions of historical continuity, for
> example, had degenerated into little more than a convenient
> formalism that guided the teachers in selecting texts for
> courses like British or American literature, disappearing almost
> completely from the enacted and received curricula. Genre
> study served a similar role in text selection, again with little
> impact on the curricular conversations that ensued. (p. 426)

Sad as it seems, this finding makes sense. Why? Both organizational schemes group works together that place very different demands on readers. We think one example can make both points. In one American Literature anthology on Michael's shelves, the works of Emily Dickinson and Walt Whitman appear consecutively in a unit titled "A National Conscience (1855–1900)." So our question becomes, How does reading Dickinson prepare one to read Whitman? Both wrote poetry, to be sure, but the nature of their poetry could hardly be more different. As a quick indication of that difference Whitman's "Song of Myself" is composed of 15,804 words, while Dickinson's "The Bustle in the House" is composed of 34. Whitman is earnest; Dickinson, ironic. Whitman is celebrated as the father of free verse; Dickinson is celebrated for her experiments with meter, rhyme, and stanza form. Although both were surely affected by the events of their time, Whitman is clearly much more explicitly political.

We could go on, but our point is simply this: How does reading Dickinson prepare a reader to read Whitman? We don't think it does. Indeed, as we've argued, such broad genre groupings as "poetry" don't serve us well. If we follow Rabinowitz (Rabinowitz & Smith, 1998) and regard genre "not as a group of texts that share textual features, but rather as a collection of texts that call on similar sets of rules, that invite similar interpretive strategies" (p. 60), then we'd have a different grouping. Think of reading selected Whitman and Allen Ginsberg poems together—for example, as part of a much more bounded genre (call it maybe oratorical poetry or some such)—and thinking with your students about how to respond to the catalogs/lists they employ in their work.

Or think of reading both in a unit built around these paired EQs: To what extent are people in a nation connected? To what extent should they be? Both poets take up this issue in their writing. Whitman's celebrations of connectedness and Ginsberg's more ambivalent attitude would provide an interesting contrast. Such a unit would provide students far better preparation for increasingly sophisticated interpretive work than would a loosely organized thematic unit with a title like "Expressions," a third organizational scheme often found in anthologies, and one in which Whitman and Ginsberg could also appear.

The different kinds of units we've mentioned aren't rigid or inflexible; they can be created and adapted to fit the needs of your students. We hope that the idea of pairing texts from the same genre in a unit built around an EQ demonstrates this flexibility. Ask how one text could prepare students to read the next, and you will likely find a variety of connections among texts that will help prepare students to have meaningful and pleasurable transactions with those texts.

3. Develop Principles of Sequencing Within and Across Units

In this chapter, we've argued for the importance of creating units that will allow students to develop knowledge text by text by making the kinds of intertextual connections that experienced readers make. Developing units requires more than identifying generative connections. It also means sequencing readings, activities, and assignments within a unit to maximize their impact. Finally, it means creating sequences of units so students can also be developing knowledge *unit by unit*.

Sequencing Within Units

We've already made an elaborated argument for the importance of developing, over time, both conceptual and strategic knowledge, so we won't repeat ourselves here. But we do want to stress that there are other sequencing decisions one needs to make in designing a unit. Once again, teachers from the Boise State Writing Project provide an excellent illustration of just what we mean.

One group of teachers began their work together by doing some reading on sequencing (e.g., Hillocks & Smith, 1988; Smith & Wilhelm, 2010; Wilhelm, Baker, & Dube, 2001). After doing so, the teachers came up with the following heuristics to help themselves think about sequencing texts and activities:

When sequencing texts within a unit, move from . . .

- Simple to more complex textual experiences

- Short to long texts

- Visual or visually supported texts to those without visual support

- Texts that are direct and literal to those that are indirect and have high inference loads

- Concrete texts to more abstract texts

- Texts closer to student experience to those that are more distant from it

When sequencing activities within a unit, move through the six *Ms* . . .

- **Motivating:** Essential questions and frontloading.

- **Modeling:** Teacher does/students watch—read-alouds, guided reading, think-alouds, drama and action strategies, visual strategies, and so on.

- **Mentoring:** Teacher does/students help and students do together and teacher helps.

- **Monitoring:** Students do together or alone/teacher watches—independent use of all strategies to complete culminating projects. Students create their own culminating projects that demonstrate their mastery and understanding in actual accomplishment.

- Using **multiple modalities**—throughout, students are assisted through various forms and modalities—use strengths to address weaknesses.

LIVINGSTON HIGH SCHOOL CURRICULUM

Threaded Unit	Influences on Perception	The Human Condition	Ideal Relationships	The Emotional Response
9th grade	How do our age and experience influence our thinking?	To what extent can you really know someone?	What makes a good friend?	What makes something tragic? (What is tragedy?)
10th grade	How do our family and/or social class influence us?	To what extent do individuals control their own lives?	What is a hero?	What makes something frightening? (What is fear? How do authors instill fear in their readers?)
11th grade	How do our time and place influence our thinking?	Is "liberty and justice" attainable for all? How can we balance everyone's rights?	What makes a good citizen?	What makes something beautiful? (What is beauty?)
12th grade	How do our gender and race influence our thinking?	What are the ingredients of a perfect world?	What makes for true love?	What makes something comedic? (What is comedy/absurdism?)

Literary Element	Character	Setting/Context	Point of View	Theme
9th grade	How character is revealed	Physical dimension	Narrator status	9—Single theme in a work
10th grade	The complexity of characters (flat vs. round)	Temporal dimension	Narrator/reader relationship	10—How motifs are used to illustrate theme
11th grade	Relationships between characters in a text	Sociopsychological	Narrator stance	11—Comparing themes in multiple texts
12th grade	Juxtaposing characters from various texts	Negotiating all three	Negotiating all three	12—Comparing themes in multiple texts by the same author

Focal Reading Skill	• Planning/monitoring • Determining importance • Asking questions	• Making inferences • Visualizing	• Making connections • Synthesizing	• Judging/critiquing

Writing Assignment	Personal Narrative	Argument/Persuasion**	Expository/Research**	Literary Analysis
9th grade	Autobiography of a discrete experience	Argument of judgment	Annotated bibliography and short research paper	Analysis of literary element
10th grade	Personal portrait to a family member	Argument of policy	Cause/effect	Compare/contrast paper

Figure 5.6

LIVINGSTON HIGH SCHOOL CURRICULUM (Continued)

Writing Assignment	Personal Narrative	Argument/ Persuasion**	Expository/Research**	Literary Analysis
11th grade	Themed autobiography of one aspect of the writer's life	Extended definition	I-Search paper	Review of literary criticism
12th grade	Memoir	Choice of argument paper**	Extended research**	Multiple works from genre/ time period

** Senior year flip-flops MP2 and MP3 writing tasks.

Genre	In addition to novels, all students will be exposed to the following genres: short stories, poems, plays, and nonfiction.
9th grade	Specifically, freshmen will be exposed to narrative poetry, mythology, newspaper articles.
10th grade	Specifically, sophomores will be exposed to ballads, epic poems, and mysteries/science fiction.
11th grade	Specifically, juniors will be exposed to an American play, free verse, and allegory.
12th grade	Specifically, seniors will be exposed to a Shakesperean play, sonnet, satire, and parody.

Grammar				
9th grade	Sentence structure (combining, fragments, run-ons) punctuating dialogue	Comparatives and superlatives	Capitalization, embedding quotations, MLA format	Punctuation (commas, end punctuation marks)/ commonly confused words
10th grade	Verb tense consistency	Subject/verb agreement	Pronoun usage (agreement, reference, case)	Parallelism
11th grade	Active/passive voice	Subordination/ coordination	MLA format plus	SAT review
12th grade	Punctuation (dash vs. semicolon vs. comma vs. parentheses)	Effective use of fragments in writing	Cumulative review	Cumulative review

Speaking/ Media Literacy	Speaking and Listening Project	Media Literacy Analysis**	Group Speaking and Listening Project**	Media Literacy Creation
9th grade	Oral declamation (of a memoir excerpt)	Debate**	Analyze news article headlines for bias**	Freshman project— children's literature
10th grade	Socratic seminar	Debate or mock trial	Analyze a website for bias	Multimedia essential question presentation
11th grade	Dramatic monologue	Analyze TV Show	Press conference/talk show/reality show	Junior project—literature in context
12th grade	Socratic seminar	Analyze TV news shows for bias	Scene performance	Senior project—themes and motifs

**Freshmen and sophomore years flip-flops MP2 and MP3 speaking and media literacy units.

- Designing **multiple measures**—throughout the unit, there are multiple ways to demonstrate progress and achievement.

Sequencing Across Units

It's also important to think about how to sequence *across* units. One way is to think about the kinds of writing students would be doing in each unit. The CCSS put great emphasis on argumentation, so, for example, writing assignments (and hence units) could be sequenced by the kinds of evidence students would need to employ, as in the following:

- Arguments in which students are likely to know evidence already

- Arguments in which students draw on evidence from single text

- Arguments in which students draw on a range of secondary sources

- Arguments in which students draw on range of primary sources

- Arguments for which students generate new data through their own data gathering and critical inquiry

The faculty members at Livingston High School provide another example of how generative discussions of sequencing can be. The faculty there worked together to sequence instruction both within and across years. This curriculum, a working document that they continuously assess and revise, seems to us to be both remarkably rich and remarkably efficient. It's outlined in Figure 5.6.

Not everyone will be able to develop such a deeply integrated curriculum. But that doesn't mean we shouldn't try. It's high time that teachers of the English language arts take sequencing as seriously as our colleagues in other disciplines. Unfortunately, the CCSS and the material that has been written to support them may well be pulling teachers away from thoughtful discussions of sequencing. If that pulling away is indeed occurring, our students will be the poorer for it, and the Standards will have, in effect, weakened rather than strengthened our students' abilities to read and interpret texts.

Aiming for Complex Interpretation 6

How to Be Street Smart About Choosing Complex Texts

We've heard a number of disquieting stories about how schools and districts are using the grade-level lists of text exemplars that are included in Appendix B of the CCSS document as curriculum guides (see National Governors Association Center for Best Practices/Council of Chief State School Officers [NGA Centers/CCSSO], 2010b). For example, at a recent panel discussion among inservice teachers that Deborah arranged for her preservice teachers, one major theme was the inservice teachers' worry that they would lose the chance to choose texts they thought would be most enjoyable and useful to their students and ones most in line with their teaching goals and instead have to draw their reading from Appendix B. In this chapter, we explain why we're so worried, but in doing so, we take a slightly different tack than we have in previous chapters. We can't blame David Coleman and the other Standards writers for such a short-sighted practice. They make it very clear that the illustrative texts listed in Appendix B "are meant only to show individual titles that are representative of a range of topics and genres." We haven't found any writing or speaking in which Coleman or his colleagues are more prescriptive.

Little wonder: That kind of prescription wouldn't make any sense. Our focus in this chapter is to explain why.

Where Interpretations of the Standards Get It Wrong

As we've noted, the power of the list of text exemplars is so great that some schools, we understand, are going so far as to attempt to purchase sets of these materials and require them for classroom use. The lists are meant to provide *examples* for teachers to explore the issue of text complexity and the kinds of text quality that the CCSS people think are appropriate for a particular grade level. This exploration, in turn, is supposed to help teachers make their own informed decisions regarding text selection. The lists are exemplars of text quality and complexity, not a required reading list!

Moreover, the developers of the list were not free to include what they thought would be the best possible exemplars. Kathy Short (2013) reports on this little-known fact:

> Because the goal of the standards group was to show text complexity, they needed to provide excerpts from each of the selected texts. One of the issues that the group encountered was getting permission to publish excerpts without paying large permission fees. An administrator from CCSSO told me that many of the texts they originally chose had to be eliminated because they could not get these permissions.

As a consequence, the authors of the CCSS document ended up having to include many dated texts that were in the public domain in order to avoid paying these permissions. Therefore, we have a list that is not a reflection of the committee's best thinking, that tends to be dated instead of contemporary, and that focuses primarily on traditional print instead of on any new media.

Maybe it's inevitable that when some kind of authority provides a list of suggestions that the list seems to possess some kind of coercive force. But this is a problem as it creates a context in which teachers and students could be restricted to books that are dated and lacking in diversity and that are not relevant to their lives, to their developing reading

The lists are exemplars of text quality and complexity, not a required reading list!

capacities, and to the context and purposes of instruction. If we really want to promote deep and engaged learning and create motivated life-long readers who can create and sustain their own reading lives and who can employ the strategies highlighted in the Core, then the last thing we need to do is limit teachers' or students' reasons for reading, materials for reading, or strategies for reading. We should not blindly adhere to what is perceived as a prescriptive list.

Moreover, there's yet another problem: The exemplars just don't mirror what the CCSS document has to say about text selection. Let's take a closer look. The "Key Points in English Language Arts" (NGA Centers/ CCSSO, 2012) provide guidelines for evaluating literature and informational texts and include the following considerations. They begin with the idea that texts must demonstrate a "staircase" of complexity and progressive development of reading comprehension. Three criteria are used to evaluate the level of text complexity: Qualitative, Quantitative, and Reader and Task.

Unfortunately, as we pointed out in last chapter, the exemplars don't model or demonstrate any principles of sequencing. They don't consider what students can already do as readers in terms of their meaning-making capacities or how what they are reading today can inform what they could do next. They don't provide rich or various examples of contemporary literature that could provide scaffolding for reading more complex texts that are more distant from students' experience. As one teacher in the Navajo Nation lamented on a blog,

> I wish they had provided more examples of diverse authors and experiences. I struggle to find texts for Native American students that reflect their experience and would be considered complex enough to read for the common core standards. Any suggestions? (Overturf, 2011)

In addition, none of the little writing elucidating the choices on the list exhibits any real consideration of the kids who will be reading them, the tasks the reading of the exemplars would help kids to accomplish, or the contexts that would make the reading of the exemplars meaningful. And although the CCSS focus on strategic understandings, Appendix B

We have an exemplar list that is not a reflection of the committee's best thinking, that tends to be dated instead of contemporary, and that focuses primarily on traditional print.

suggests content without a consideration of how this material will assist students to master the strategies foregrounded in the anchor standards.

Three Ways to Choose the Right Books for Your Kids

So if the exemplars don't work, what should we do instead? We have three suggestions.

1. Work With Other Teachers on Selecting Texts

Teaching Fellows from the Boise State Writing Project provide a model of the kind of collaboration we're calling for. The group began by reading the National Council of Teachers of English (NCTE) standards for text and material selection, which they summarized as follows:

- Texts must be connected to educational objectives; that is, texts are part of an integrated and coherent instructional whole.

- Texts must be relevant to students and their learning needs by drawing on and then extending students' knowledge and interests.

- Texts must be appropriately challenging and applicable in a context of use.

Through collaborative discussion, the group fleshed out what these bullet points mean. They determined that texts should not be an end in themselves but, rather, should be selected in terms of the unit context and goals of a particular unit; of student capacities, interests, and needs; and of the logic of the sequence of instructional scaffolding and assistance. In other words, the teachers determined that they should ask themselves what texts would help students deal with particular concepts, strategies, and perspectives and how learning those concepts and strategies might lead to success with other texts and learning challenges. The group agreed that texts operate best in conversation with other texts and spent quite a bit of time thinking about how particular texts and their construction positioned or repositioned readers.

At the second meeting, they came up with the guide to text selection featured in Box 6.1.

Overall Goal

To inspire reflective behavior and questioning; to promote deep understanding and application of what is learned both conceptually and strategically; to lead children to read widely and enthusiastically inside but especially outside of school.

Considerations

1. How will the selected texts promote motivation, engagement, and the continuing impulse to read and learn?

2. How will the texts address different students' interests, capacities, and needs, their varying motivational and strategic "zones of proximal development"?

3. How will the texts help students grapple with engaging problems related to our unit level inquiry?

   a. What important concepts and ideas will students be asked to deal with by the text?

   b. How will students be positioned and repositioned by the texts to deal with these issues?

4. What strategies will students have to learn or consolidate to read and respond to the text?

A GUIDE TO TEXT SELECTION

Box 6.1

The group maintained that thinking about texts in these ways helped them put their students at the center, while still considering the qualitative, quantitative, and reader and task considerations of particular texts and how these related to unit goals. This, in turn, helped the teachers think about providing texts that were rewarding in the moment and truly complex for students—and not just difficult for the sake of being difficult.

At their third meeting, the group worked to articulate criteria for their various considerations and ended up with the checklist in Box 6.2.

MOTIVATION AND INTEREST CHECKLIST

The Text . . .

☐ Provides a motivating and meaningful challenge that is immediately interesting to students

☐ Is highly engaging, thought provoking, energizing, and compelling to students

☐ Deals with issues related to student interests and their evolving understandings of themselves and the world, and that they perceive as relevant as related to the unit inquiry

☐ Will position and reposition the readers so that they deal with multiple perspectives and will therefore deepen understanding

☐ Leads to practical applications in students' everyday lives

☐ Provides ongoing and visible signs of accomplishment as readers, learners, and citizens

Conceptual, Strategic, and Ethical Growth

☐ Elicits personal, thoughtful, critical responses to the unit inquiry

☐ Promotes dialogic sharing and conversation—with author, characters, and other students

☐ Broadens student understanding conceptually, procedurally, and in terms of becoming a tolerant democratic citizen capable of taking multiple perspectives

☐ Connects to and challenges students current thinking

☐ Promotes nuanced ethical considerations of real issues

☐ Uses language that is essential to the work and uses it powerfully, responsibly, and thoughtfully for meaning and effect

☐ Introduces students to ideas and concepts and perspectives they likely have not been exposed to; may confront misconceptions

Box 6.2

The guides in these two boxes were written by one group of teachers thoughtfully dealing with the issue of how to select texts. By working together, the Teaching Fellows provided much more guidance than the minimal amount the CCSS document does. The CCSS document says that there should be qualitative considerations of text complexity that include analyses of "levels of meaning, structure, language conventionality and clarity, and knowledge demands" (NGA Centers/CCSSO, 2010a, p. 57). The document also encourages teachers to consider "reader variables (such as motivation, knowledge, and experiences) and task variables (such as purpose and the complexity generated by the task assigned and the questions posed)" (p. 57). But the document does not provide guidance about *how* to do so. This is where the teachers stepped in to fill the gap.

The takeaway from these teachers? Choosing the right text to teach depends on a number of things beyond simply the *content* of the text:

- An awareness of one's own positions—that is, one's ideological stance on and current thinking about the topic and/or text at hand

- The positions we want students to move through

- The positions of the local and disciplinary communities we want students to contend with

- The concepts and strategies that we want students to learn

- The resulting motivation and continuing impulse to read and learn that we want the reading selections to cultivate

- The interests and abilities of the students—and, even more, their *potential* interests and capacities

Thinking hard about text selection is facilitated by thoughtful and collaborative discussions.

2. Think Hard About the Benefits Different Kinds of Texts Provide

Contemporary Literature

As we've noted, Appendix B of the CCSS (NGA Centers/CCSSO, 2010b) is made up primarily of canonical literary and nonliterary texts. As

Deborah (Appleman, 2006) has noted, "Despite recent attempts to diversify and contemporize what we teach, many secondary students fail to encounter books written since they were born in their literature curricula" (p. 4). If teachers use Appendix B as a curriculum guide, students will seldom encounter books written since even their parents were born. Indeed, of the 39 exemplar texts in the table on page 58 of the Standards document (NGA Centers/CCSSO, 2010a), only two were written since 1975 and most of them way, way before that.

When Deborah (Appleman, 2006) cofounded a before-school book club in which students and teachers met to talk about their reading, she and her colleagues used eight criteria to select texts. They chose books with these characteristics:

- Current

- Playful

- Discussible

- Creating a buzz in the culture at large

- Able to connect adults and kids

- Able to appeal to men and women

- Available in paperback form

- Able to push literary boundaries

Something worked. Here are students talking about *The Tao of Pooh*, the very first book discussed at the very first meeting:

Student 1:   Well, I really enjoyed, like on page 112 of the same chapter that talks about how "enjoyment of the process is the secret that erases the myths of the Great Reward and Saving Time." It just like shows, like, every year we go through Christmas and you just anticipate the gifts, but then once it's over you're just back where you started. But that anticipation is the part that is the most fun. So it's kind of not necessarily the reward, but the time before it. I like that idea.

Like everyone just goes through high school and tries to get good grades, so that they can get into a good college. But high school is four years of your life that you could be enjoying. Obviously, that doesn't stop you from enjoying necessarily, but if you *focused* more on enjoying the process of your life . . . That doesn't mean don't work, but it just means, like, enjoy where you are right now. I think, you know, that people would be a lot happier.

Student 2: I thought Katie brought up an interesting point about how [the author] shows contrast between Pooh and the Chinese proverbs. On pages 68 and 69 when he's talking about the Wu Wei, he says, "Literally, Wu Wei means without doing, causing, or making," and then he kind of talks about that. Then, right at the bottom, he says, "Let's take an example from the writing of Chuang-Tse," and then right after that on the next page he goes, "Now look at the most effortless bear we've ever seen" and then he goes through examples of Pooh. I think it's cool how he can, like, show the contrast and show the parallels between those two. I think it's interesting.

Student 3: Well, what you were saying about high school, I thought that was one of the most interesting things too. And my favorite passage was, "'It is today, sweet Piglet, my favorite day' says Pooh" and that every day could be his favorite day. And he just enjoys it. That would be incredible to embrace, and that's what I like best about the book. (Appleman, 2006, pp. 35–36)

This excerpt suggests that the book fostered just the kind of instructional conversation that we admire. Note the interplay between careful attention to the text and making connections between the text and the reader's lives. Note how they were listening to each other. Note how fully they developed their ideas. Note how they were meeting multiple Core

Standards for reading, speaking, and listening, as well as for composing meaning. And note that The *Tao of Pooh* is not listed as an exemplar.

Diverse Formats and Media

As powerful as books can be, to meet the needs of various students and to meet the CCSS's call to "integrate and evaluate content presented in diverse formats and media" (NGA Centers/CCSSO, 2010a, p. 35), teachers need to go beyond traditional print texts. This standard resonates with a very influential argument made by the New London Group (1996), which was among the first to call for curricula to include attention to visual, audio, gestural, spatial, and multimodal meanings

Let's look closely at the first alternative they provide: visual meanings. Graphic novels are among the genres that employ visual meanings. Our recent research into the nature and variety of pleasure students take from their out-of-school reading (Wilhelm & Smith, 2014) has convinced us of the importance and power of these meanings. Look at how Rori, a committed reader of graphic novels, responded to a series of questions by Jeff:

J: Now, do you, are you the kind of reader who looks really hard at the pictures and how they're drawn and what's in there?

R: The first time I read a book I usually just kind of skim through it and then I'll read it a couple of times and the second time I'll read it, I'll read it for the words and the story, but usually about the third time I read it I'll look at the pictures and I'll look how, I'll look at the visuals the third time I read it.

J: So you're attending to different things every time through so you're getting different things. Now would you read a fantasy novel in the same way? How is rereading a graphic novel different?

R: By rereading a graphic novel you have more to look over cuz there's just words in let's say a novel and you can either skim those words or read those words, but in graphic novels you have words and pictures so you can either skim those pictures and get the main idea or you can look at the details and the other things about that. (Wilhelm & Smith, 2014, p. 80)

Sharon, our research assistant on the project, talked about how much she leaned from Rori about the potential power of visual texts:

> She has elevated the graphic novel for me. Previously, I would
> have said that graphic novels were more of a form for kids
> who aren't strong readers or who don't like to read. She makes
> a case for why they are more complex than straight novels
> and how the visuals can lead to more intellectual work than
> novels. (Wilhelm & Smith, 2014, p. 81)

Rori wasn't alone in articulating the intellectual pleasure she took from graphic novels. Here's Paul:

J: Right, are there any other pictures in here that you really, really like that are worth talking about?

P: That was in the beginning. Right here, this picture I thought was interesting because there's a ton going on. Tintin's woken up from a dream and he yells a name and everybody's going crazy and there's champagne glasses and cigarettes and coffee and all sorts of stuff flying. Like there's a little puzzle in the background and I appreciate the scene because it must have taken forever to draw this. It's got a ton of people doing a ton of things. I like a scene in a graphic novel where it will do that, but then you've got to explain it in other panels like right here.

J: So do you spend some time kind of looking at it, studying it, going back to it?

P: Yeah, like my friends will kind of blow through a comic book or a graphic novel or something and I'll just be going slow and they'll be wondering what's up with me because I like to look at most of the details in the pictures like even in these small panels he has a picture on the wall and he drew the picture very detailed like right there he's got the picture on the wall. (Wilhelm & Smith, 2014, p. 81)

Once again we see the lesson that Radway (1984) taught in her foundational research on the responses of working-class women to romances: *You can't understand how texts work unless you understand how readers engage with them.* And texts that seem uncomplicated on their surface can foster serious intellectual work.

Of course, it's not just visual texts that provide the occasion for significant interpretive work. Morrell (2002) and Hill (2009) are among those who have documented how a hip-hop curriculum can, in Hill's words, engage young people in becoming "cultural critics who deploy[ed] critical literacies in order to identify and respond to structures of power and meaning within hip-hop texts" (p. 122).

Appendix B (NGA Centers/CCSSO, 2010b) doesn't list any of these alternative forms of texts. We think it should. Since it does not, it is up to us as teachers, with other teachers, library media specialists, and our students, to come up with lists and libraries of the kinds of alternative texts that will fit in our units, be compelling as free-choice reading, and work both toward the CCSS and toward our bigger goals as teachers to create engaged, competent, critical, lifelong readers.

3. Think About *Interpretive* Complexity, Not Just Text Complexity

Our third suggestion is closely tied with our second. The more you pay attention to how kids engage with different kinds of texts, the more you'll be astonished by just what they do with them. If you pay attention, you'll recognize that interpretive complexity is not a function of textual complexity.

Bancroft and Rabinowitz (2013) provide a succinct summary of the fundamental point we want to make in this section:

> Coleman argues that "The real distinction in the growth
> of reading is *of course* the level of complexity of the text
> that you're managing" (10) (emphasis added). Of course,
> Coleman's "of course" is intended to brush aside objections
> before they are raised, but we'll raise ours anyway. For us,
> what's significant is not the complexity of the text, but the
> complexity of the interpretive act you're performing. (p. 4)

And extraordinarily complex interpretive work can be encouraged with what the CCSS and Appendix B would define as less complex texts.

Throughout our careers, both as teachers and researchers, we've learned from our students and student-informants not to underestimate what they already know and do as readers and writers. Text complexity, as conceived in the CCSS, doesn't credit the complex work that kids already do with other kinds of texts, texts they might already love to read. When Jeff studied middle school readers in *You Gotta BE the Book* (Wilhelm, 2008), he was astonished at the complexity of his students' interpretive moves. He coded 10 dimensions of their responses to literature, running from evocative to connective to reflective classes of response. There were multiple strategies used in every dimension. He further found that he could use activities like think-alouds, visual strategies, and drama to get the more expert readers in his classes to name and share their expertise with less expert readers in ways that they could appropriate and subsequently use on their own, making the more expert students into the modelers, mentors, and monitors of other students' learning.

Similarly, in Jeff and Michael's most recent study, *Reading Unbound* (Wilhelm & Smith, 2014), they found that students who were passionate readers of marginalized texts enjoyed varieties of intense pleasures with these texts and also did significant kinds of intellectual, functional, and inner work through their reading of these texts. A few examples from readers of young adult dystopian novels, of which no examples appear in Appendix B, make the point quite clearly.

For Michelle, one of our participants, dystopias are extrapolations of current trends and predictions about the future: "Like if humankind goes one way, then we'll end up like *The Hunger Games*" (Wilhelm & Smith, 2014, p. 156). She also saw such books as cultural and societal critiques, particularly of authority and government, and a call to be wide awake and distrustful of the status quo: Dystopias were always about "government oppression." She found such books to be "terribly exciting," partly because of their realism and their implications for her current thinking and action.

Paul, a fan of "sci-fi dystopias," agreed that dystopias are critiques of authority, society, and government: "*1984*, you can bring that into politics. Also there is if you want something [about a] flawed government or something like that read a few of the Douglass Adams [sci-fi] books because they have some politics in it" (Wilhelm & Smith, 2014, p. 162).

Extraordinarily complex interpretive work can be encouraged with what the CCSS and Appendix B would define as less complex texts.

Jazzy maintained that it is up to the dystopian book to explore "how society has come to be so bad, so unjust, or just plain stupid" (Wilhelm & Smith, 2014, p. 161). She went on the give a specific example:

> In the series the *Uglies*, the big problem is pressure about looks, and these crazy cultural notions about what's beautiful or normal . . . but in every case there is some underlying cause that has to be taken care of. (p. 161)

Ecotopian novels, for instance "look at environmental problems that are screwing us up" (p. 153).

Jazzy continued to explain that dystopias often "pay a lot of attention to technology and what it is doing to us and how it can be misused" (p. 161). Technology, or the lack of it, "seems pretty important in almost all dystopian books" (p. 161). There is an exploration of the meaning and ethics of various technologies—who has access and how technologies are used and abused:

> *The Hunger Games* is really big on exploring how technology is used to oppress people—it's kind of like *1984* that way [in the way people are monitored by technology], and about questioning reality TV, about how technology disconnects us and desensitizes us—which is kind of the opposite of how lots of people like to think about technology—as connecting us and all good. (p. 161)

These adolescent students are deeply engaged, and as far as we can see, are meeting the CCSS anchor standards for reading (see NGA Centers/ CCSSO, 2010a) with their free-choice reading. Look at the first three anchor standards:

> 1. Read closely to determine what the text says explicitly and to make logical inferences from it; cite specific textual evidence when writing or speaking to support conclusions drawn from the text.
>
> 2. Determine central ideas or themes of a text and analyze their development; summarize the key supporting details and ideas.

3. Analyze how and why individuals, events, and ideas
develop and interact over the course of a text.

All three readers seem to us to be working hard to meet all three standards. Notice, too, how they make connections from their books to classic books like *1984* that they have read in school. We'd argue that the wide reading of dystopia allowed them to make much more of *1984* and do more complex work with it. In so doing, they are meeting an additional standard:

9. Analyze how two or more texts address similar themes
or topics in order to build knowledge or to compare the
approaches the authors take.

Similarly, when Deborah studied the students' responses in her book club study, she found that students robustly met all three standards while forming the lifelong habit of reading books voluntarily and discussing them authentically, which after all, is among our primary goals as literacy educators. For example, they read closely and often cited passages from the text (with no teacher prompting) to support their interpretations (Anchor Standard 1). Whether they were discussing *The Tao of Pooh, The Kite-Runner,* or *Montana 1948,* they discovered central themes that permeated the texts (Anchor Standard 2). They also spoke passionately about individual characters, tracing their changes throughout the text (Anchor Standard 3).

In short, an emphasis on text complexity without a concomitant emphasis on interpretive complexity leaves the reader out of the equation—something that the Core descriptions of text complexity say they are trying not to do. Failing to consider interpretive complexity also seems to us to make sensible sequencing that much harder to do—since we necessarily instruct in ways that meet kids where they are and then use their current resources and interests to help them build new strategies and understandings. Further, *not* considering interpretive complexity reinforces unwarranted distinctions between the reading students do in and out of school, marginalizing what students choose to read on their own despite the fact that such reading often works powerfully—in many instances more powerfully than in-school reading—to meet the goals that the Core articulates.

Moreover, the list of exemplars without any consideration of the instructional leverage they provide, or the contexts in which they might provide it, seems to us to be at odds with the strategic emphasis of the CCSS and at odds with how people actually develop and grow as readers. The exemplars focus on the qualities and content of specific texts instead of on the cultivation of student strategies—and strategies are what all the anchor standards highlight and require.

As we noted earlier, some educators have read Appendix B (NGA Centers/CCSSO, 2010b) as a mandate to "teach these texts." We have to remember that we can use less complex texts in any instructional sequence to motivate, develop, and consolidate the strategies that the CCSS foregrounds and to move students toward the interest and capacities of reading more complex texts.

When we think about selecting texts, we should be asking,

- What texts help us do our work conceptually in a particular unit so that students achieve deep understanding?

- What texts situate, invite, and reward the strategic activities we want students to develop?

- What texts will motivate our students so that they are willing to do the complex interpretive work we want them to do?

A list devoid of any thoughtful discussion of kids and contexts invites misuse. It's crucial that teachers work together to resist that misuse. Instead, we need to move sensibly toward meeting the CCSS even as we work to reach even higher goals of creating highly proficient, critical, and lifelong readers who find great pleasure in reading and talking about texts.

> The list of exemplars without any consideration of the instructional leverage they provide, or the contexts in which they might provide it, seems to be at odds with the strategic emphasis of the CCSS and with how people actually develop and grow as readers.

Putting Our Money Where Our Mouths Are 7

Our Unit for Teaching "Letter From Birmingham Jail"

Throughout this book, we have been criticizing the instructional ideas of the authors of the Common Core State Standards (CCSS) for their narrow New Critical focus, for their apparent failure to recognize how a focus on the text can be supported by a focus beyond the text, for their apparent failure to recognize the importance of developing prior knowledge, for their apparent failure to encourage developing strategic understandings that can be transferred from text to text, and for the absence of any serious attention to the power of instructional sequencing. We've also discussed how misunderstandings about the text complexity standard and the text exemplars may lead to impoverished curricula.

Throughout this book, we've also offered research-based instructional ideas that we believe hold more promise for meeting the CCSS than do the instructional ideas of the Standards writers themselves. In order to summarize our arguments, in this chapter we look closely at the instructional plan that David Coleman proposes for teaching King's "Letter From Birmingham Jail" and contrast it with the kind of instruction that we'd advocate, which we provide for you in a unit plan, lesson by lesson.

David Coleman on King's "Letter"

Let's start by taking a close look at how Coleman advocates teaching King's "Letter." We're going to draw on the transcript of "Bringing the Common Core to Life," the presentation he made before the New York State Department of Education on April 28, 2011 (Coleman, 2011) to do so.

We've already discussed Coleman's position on pre-reading, so it's no surprise that he'd want to start with the "Letter" itself. He implies that he'd ask students to read the first paragraph and that after they had done so, he'd read it aloud. Then he'd begin whole-class, teacher-directed discussion with this question: "Based on this text and this text alone, what do you know? What can you make out about the letter King received?" He explains that "clever" students might notice that King himself must be a clergyman but then explains that "we can already know at least two things, it's written to clergymen and says you've been unwise and untimely." This first question reveals the approach he takes throughout his modeling: asking a series of his text-dependent questions that have single correct answers.

> Coleman's first question reveals the approach he takes throughout: asking a series of text-dependent questions that have single correct answers.

That approach is repeated as students (played by the teachers in his audience; we'd love to see him do the same lesson with actual students) march through the "Letter." They read paragraphs 2 through 4 and he asks, "What are the three very different arguments King makes for why he's in Birmingham? And what different kinds of evidence does he use to support them?" Once again he explains the answers he wants to receive. The first argument, he says, is bureaucratic; the second, religious/historical; the third, moral. He says it'd be okay for teachers to pause and explain the historical and religious references, but it's not essential because "as much as they understand that King is comparing himself now to a prophet and making a very different kind of argument, we have enough to keep moving through his argument."

Paragraph 4 introduces King's argument on what King called the "interrelatedness of all communities and states." Coleman suggests asking what could be an authentic question: "What is the force of [the moral argument]? How does it relate to the arguments that come before?" But he says that ultimately students should understand that it doesn't fit and that King doesn't present any evidence in support of it. Coleman explains that the moment students "realize as powerful as these words are that they don't yet have any support or proof is a wonderful one."

Coleman then walks his audience quickly through what he'd do with the other sections of the "Letter": paragraph 5, a transitional paragraph; paragraphs 6 through 9, what Coleman calls the "just the facts" section; paragraph 10, where the focus is on what King means by the word "tension" and why that was such a good rhetorical choice; paragraphs 15 through 21, where King makes a distinction between just and unjust laws. He doesn't say what he'd suggest for the remaining paragraphs, of the letter, including paragraphs 11 through 14, where King responds to the critique that his action are untimely, except to say that the methodical approach he is suggesting would take six days of class to complete.

Such focused attention, Coleman says, is important:

> What the world needs most right now is wonderful questions
> about things worth reading. Things worth reading and
> rereading that don't avoid the text but bring kids into a deeper
> consideration of it. You noticed I did a lot of chunking and
> reading out loud, taking a smaller portion and looking at it
> with care. That allows a much wider range of kids into that
> process. I am aware that sometimes certain kids will connect
> to more of this or less of this. Some will see more. But the
> important deep idea is that they're all part of it. And the
> wonderful thing is sometimes a kid [who] is behind will notice
> something another kid didn't. And since you're all looking
> at the same thing, you have that remarkable moment both
> as a teacher and as another reader where you say, "Ooh, I
> didn't see that. I didn't notice that," which is, by the way,
> how kids talk about a movie when they've seen it. Did you
> catch that? Did you see that? Did you watch that? Did you

see it when he did this? You notice how lively the academic vocabulary is. While we can explain Greco Roman [and] other technical terms that are academic, a rich word like tension is so powerful. (p. 23)

After those six days, Coleman says it would be appropriate to move beyond the letter, to accept King's invitation to apply his principles of justice and injustice to other laws, both those cited in the letter and other historical examples. The letter, he said, would also be a wonderful opportunity to learn about Socrates, to whom King twice alludes. Coleman says "in that third week of instruction . . . maybe it would be fun to find out who this Socrates guy was and see how he thought about tension in Athens" (p. 22). But he provides little detail about just how he sees the instruction that goes beyond the letter proceeding.

We've already presented our worries about the kind of classroom discourse Coleman advocates and we'll leave it to you to assess how your students would respond to six days of it. But before we move onto how we'd teach the letter, let's think about what students would take from such instruction. The few students who entered class already prepared to read the letter may finish the lesson understanding the letter, at least as Coleman understands it. And a few students might recognize Coleman's appreciation of the letter, though their own appreciation would, we think, be undercut by the monotony of the lesson. But so much more could be achieved.

An Alternative Approach: Our Unit for Teaching the "Letter"

We think that the alternative approaches we've discussed throughout this book offer the promise of providing students with much more, including much deeper and transferable understandings of both the procedures highlighted in the Core and the critical concepts the letter takes up. The unit we share is designed to provide those additional benefits.

A Sample Unit

"Letter From Birmingham Jail"

THE PURPOSE

How would we start? As we argued in Chapter 5, the place to start thinking about teaching any text is the instructional context in which you'd situate that teaching. We also argued that inquiry units built around essential questions are the most powerful and meaningful instructional contexts one can create. One of the ways to create those units, we argued, was to think hard about what makes a required text worth teaching.

The teachers in Jeff's courses weren't satisfied with just developing reading and writing skills in service of pursuing the inquiry and comprehending the "Letter." After a lively discussion, here's what they wanted students to do in the course of the unit:

- Exceed the skills articulated in the Common Core

- Work toward service, social action, and civil rights in their own classrooms

- Apply what they learn to their present circumstances and current local, national, and global events

Here are some of the comments they made as they talked about purpose and outcomes for students:

> This is about rehearsing and then acting out the principles of democracy. (Whitney Douglass)

> It's about cultivating habits of mind, of seeing from different perspectives, of being willing to represent yourself and others. (Sara Fry)

> We have to integrate real-life concerns into our teaching and then help kids to apply what they have learned to their lives in ways that make a difference to themselves and to others. (Sam Mora)

> This is not just about helping kids be better readers and writers. I want to work towards systemic change, towards service and democracy. (Lynne Doucette)

Inquiry means that you are solving a problem in your classroom, school, or community as you teach towards the Core standards in literacy. (Emily Morgan)

THE ESSENTIAL QUESTION

You can do this hard thinking by yourself, with your students, or with a group of teachers who will be teaching the same unit. Jeff's in-service teachers came up with these:

- When is it justifiable to resist authority?

- What would you be willing to do to get your rights?

- What are the most influential speeches/writing leading to social change? What is it about these texts that leads to change?

- What are our civil rights, and how can we best protect and promote them?

- When should/must we stand up against injustice?

- What people most need their civil rights promoted, and how can we work for this?

- What is fair? How can fairness be achieved?

- How can we achieve civil rights against powerful interests and forces?

Narrow It Down to One Question

For the purposes of this unit, we'll use this one:

- How can we achieve civil rights against powerful interests and forces?

THE ADDITIONAL TEXTS

What additional texts would encourage your students to engage deeply with the above question and prepare them to read King's "Letter?" The selections you choose will depend on your own students' interests and abilities. Remember, the texts should provide a variety of different responses to the essential question. Here are the texts that Jeff's teachers recommended, being mindful of their kids and the need for multiple perspectives:

David and Goliath by Malcolm Gladwell

"Montgomery Boycott" by Coretta Scott King

"A Chip of Glass Ruby" by Nadine Gordimer

"Black Men and Public Spaces" by Brent Staples

"As the Night the Day" by Abioseh Nicol

Farwell to Manzanar by Jeanne Wakatsuki and James Houston

"The Prisoner Who Wore Glasses" by Bessie Head

Kaffir Boy by Mark Mathabane

"Cranes" by Hwang Sunwon

UN Universal Declaration on Universal Human Rights

PRE-READING ACTIVITIES

Following are some options we do with our students. We want to point out that these activities are substantive, both conceptually and strategically. The activities were created to activate and build on students' background knowledge. They provide a situation that assists students in developing a wide variety of strategies required by the Core and then rewards them for developing those strategies. They prepare students to have meaningful transactions with a wide variety of texts, including "Letter From Birmingham Jail."

Strategic Pre-Reading Activity

- Who's on the Other Side? (see Figure 4.3 on page 88)

Conceptual Pre-Reading Activities

- Agree or Disagree? (Figure 7.1)
- Who Has the Power? (Figure 7.2)
- Reflecting on Power and Persuasion (Figure 7.3)

"AGREE OR DISAGREE?"

The "Agree or Disagree" activity presented in Figure 7.1 was developed by teacher Bonnie Warne, a high school teacher.

AGREE OR DISAGREE?

NAME: _____ DATE: _____

For each quotation, please indicate whether you Agree (A) or Disagree (D) with the statement:

_____ 1. "I'm really very sorry for you all, but it's an unjust world, and virtue is triumphant only in theatrical performances." (W. S. Gilbert, *The Mikado*)

_____ 2. "You just need to be a flea against injustice. Enough committed fleas biting strategically can make even the biggest dog uncomfortable and transform even the biggest nation." (Marian Wright Edelman)

_____ 3. "Justice is my being allowed to do whatever I like. Injustice is whatever prevents my doing so." (Samuel Johnson)

_____ 4. "Some things you must always be unable to bear. Some things you must never stop refusing to bear. Injustice and outrage and dishonor and shame. No matter how young you are or how old you have got. Not for kudos and not for cash: your picture in the paper nor money in the bank either. Just refuse to bear them." (William Faulkner, *Intruder in the Dust*)

_____ 5. "I guess the only time most people think about injustice is when it happens to them." (Charles Bukowski, *Ham on Rye*)

_____ 6. "It takes great courage to open one's heart and mind to the tremendous injustice and suffering in our world." (Vincent A. Gallagher, *The True Cost of Low Prices: The Violence of Globalization*)

_____ 7. "Do not make the mistake of thinking that you have to agree with people and their beliefs to defend them from injustice." (Bryant McGill, *Voice of Reason*)

Figure 7.1

AGREE OR DISAGREE? (Continued)

NAME: _____ DATE: _____

_____ 8. "When you take a stand against injustice inflicted upon innocent people, there will be those who will hate you for it." (Ellen J. Barrier)

_____ 9. "Injustice in the end produces independence." (Voltaire)

_____ 10. "I am a person who is unhappy with things as they stand. We cannot accept the world as it is. Each day we should wake up foaming at the mouth because of the injustice of things." (Hugo Claus)

_____ 11. "It's hard not to empathize with the mayor's anger, given the injustices he'd suffered, but righteous anger rarely leads to wise policy." (Edward L. Glaeser, *Triumph of the City: How Our Greatest Invention Makes Us Richer, Smarter, Greener, Healthier, and Happier*)

_____ 12. "In the beginning there was only a small amount of injustice abroad in the world, but everyone who came afterwards added their portion, always thinking it was very small and unimportant, and look where we have ended up today." (Paulo Coelho, *The Devil and Miss Prym*)

_____ 13. "Each time a man stands up for an ideal, or acts to improve the lot of others, or strikes out against injustice, he sends forth a tiny ripple of hope, and those ripples build a current which can sweep down the mightiest walls of oppression and resistance." (Robert F. Kennedy)

_____ 14. "I believe that our identity is at risk. That when we don't actually care about these difficult things, the positive and wonderful things are nonetheless implicated. We love innovation, we love technology, we love creativity, we love entertainment—but ultimately those realities are shadowed by suffering, abuse, degradation, marginalization. . . . We will not be fully human until we connect with injustice." (Bryan Stevenson)

FOLLOW-UP TO "AGREE OR DISAGREE" ACTIVITY

Small-Group Work. Students discuss their responses in small groups, identifying the claim or claims in each quote and what evidence might be provided in support.

Optional. To link this activity to the strategic pre-reading activity, "Who's on the Other Side?" ask students to discuss what quotes provide counterclaims to other quotes. The students then choose two of the quotes from the "Agree or Disagree" activity and write mini-arguments, providing evidence that supports the quote's claim (what I have to go on/what makes me say so) and explaining how that evidence linked to the claim (so what?).

The preceding activities activate students' interest in and knowledge of injustice and how to combat it and also build upon that knowledge as students share views through discussion and exchange of ideas. At the same time the activities provide procedural scaffolding in evidence-based reasoning and argumentation, which students will be called upon to employ in this unit's culminating writing assignment. In short, students get lots of conceptual and procedural frontloading that will assist them later in both their reading and their writing. (See Smith, Wilhelm, & Fredricksen, 2012, for a full discussion of such activities for teaching argument.)

"WHO HAS THE POWER?"

The following activity, "Who Has the Power?" shown in Figure 7.2, engages students in thinking about who has power to enact change.

Once again, after engaging in this activity, students should share the responses they felt most strongly about and write a short argument justifying their response by providing evidence (what I have to go on/what makes me say so) and explaining how that evidence linked to the claim (so what?).

"REFLECTING ON POWER AND PERSUASION"

The next activity (Figure 7.3) encourages students to reflect on their own experience in ways that will help them use that experience as a resource when they are reading.

WHO HAS THE POWER?

NAME: _____ DATE: _____

Check the group or individual in each pair who you think has more capacity to enact change. Be prepared to explain what makes you say so and why—that is, "so what" (data and reasoning).

___ The President	OR	___ Bill Gates
___ Pitcher	OR	___ Batter
___ Women	OR	Men
___ Actor	OR	___ Script
___ Parent	OR	___ You
___ President of the student body	OR	___ Editor of the school newspaper
___ Friendship	OR	___ Family
___ Internet	OR	___ TV
___ Love	OR	___ Hate
___ Police officer	OR	___ Judge
___ Comedian	OR	___ Politician
___ Armed forces	OR	___ Citizens
___ Paintings	OR	___ Photographs argument
___ Protest music	OR	___ Published argument

Figure 7.2

REFLECTING ON POWER AND PERSUASION

NAME: _____ DATE: _____

Complete these sentences in any way that rings true for you:

1. I feel strong when _____ because _____.

2. I feel weak when _____ because _____.

3. People with power should _____ because _____.

4. People being oppressed should _____ because _____.

5. I'm most persuasive when _____ because _____.

6. I'm least persuasive when _____ because _____.

7. The most powerful person is _____ because _____.

8. The least powerful person is _____ because _____.

Figure 7.3

FOLLOW-UP TO "REFLECTING ON POWER AND PERSUASION" ACTIVITY

Whole-Class Discussion. After completing their forms, we reconvene as a class and discuss the statements students wrote. We help them identify the potential for social action in response to injustice and consider the responses to injustice made by the people about whom they will be reading. We practice using the evidence and reasoning that are necessary to making an effective argument.

Reinforce the Purpose: Create an Anchor Chart. We suggest regularly reminding students of the essential question and the purpose of the unit: *How can we work toward change and civil rights when opposed by powerful interests and forces?*

One way we do this is to create an anchor chart labeled "What can help us overcome powerful forces?" We remind students that this was the situation that Dr. King found himself in throughout his lifetime of work toward civil rights and that we will soon be reading a text that he used in the struggle to achieve civil rights for African Americans and other minorities. As we read, we begin filling in the chart.

READING THE TEXTS

• Day 1

Reading. Read "Introduction" to Gladwell's (2013) *David and Goliath* in class together with students in which Gladwell proclaims that the book is about what happens "when ordinary people confront giants. By 'giants' I mean powerful opponents of all kinds— from armies and mighty warriors to disability, misfortune, and oppression" (p. 5).

Whole-Class Work. The class ponders the reading and lists the "giants" that oppose equality and the achievement of civil rights in Dr. King's time and in our own.

Pair Work. Students work in pairs to identify strengths and resources that "less powerful" people or groups might have in the struggle for civil rights.

Whole Class. Pairs report back and class begins listing strengths and resources on the anchor chart.

[Jeff's students' list included the following: courage, faith, belief in your cause, knowing your strengths, knowing the strengths of the opponent, knowing your own and your opponent's weaknesses, knowing that your strengths can be your weaknesses, and relentlessly pressing all advantages.]

• Day 2

Reading. The class reads Chapter 1 of Gladwell's book about the realization that came to software mogul Vivak Renadive while coaching his daughter's basketball team: Underdogs had to acknowledge their weaknesses and choose an unconventional strategy to compete because convention favors the powerful. The reading could be assigned or done in class through paired partner reading.

Whole-Class Work. We begin with a whole-group brainstorming session during which students begin to list resources for fighting the powers in the status quo that might be oppressive.

Pair Work. In pairs, students add to the list of resources for fighting the powers in the status quo that might be oppressive. Here are just some of the things our students came up with:

- Questioning the status quo
- Breaking the unwritten rules
- Sharing the load
- Taking the offensive
- Choosing the ground
- Using fake-outs and surprise
- Hiding weaknesses and playing to strengths
- Planning, practicing, and being tight and cooperative with your team

Reading. Students individually read selections about how to combat cyberbullying, taken from Glen Downey's (2014) *Digital World*. Ask them to compare the resources needed to combat cyberbullying to their ongoing anchor chart list. Add to the list as students see fit.

Reading. Students read several trickster tales told by oppressed peoples, including several Anansi and Coyote tales. (When Jeff taught the unit, students self-selected print or picture book versions from the classroom library and read them in class, but the reading could also be a homework assignment. If you don't have the tales, you can find them at a variety of websites.) Again, students add to the anchor chart list.

By now, students are building a theory about what is necessary to fight for civil rights. As they work on the chart they consider this: The extent of what underdogs need to do is a function of the specific context in which they find themselves.

• Day 3

Reading. Students read Chapter 6 of *David and Goliath*, a chapter that is point on for reading the "Letter" as it is about Walker Wyatt, one of Dr. King's right-hand men in waging the civil rights struggle in Birmingham.

Read Aloud. Read aloud the first five paragraphs of M. L. King's "Letter From Birmingham Jail."

Small-Group Work. Students try to reconstruct, as best they can, the letter to which King was *responding*. [This activity asks students to apply the understandings they developed through the strategic frontloading activity we present in Figure 4.3.]

Small "Jigsaw" Group Work. Students from different groups form new groups and do the following:

1. Share their reconstructed letters and discuss the similarities and differences among them.

2. Return to the injustice quotes frontloading activity and select which quotes they think King's audience (the men who wrote him the letter he is responding to) would most strongly agree with and those with which they'd most strongly disagree.

3. Groups present their conclusions to the class.

- **Day 4**

Read Aloud. M. L. King's "Letter From Birmingham Jail": paragraphs 6–11

This is the section in which King explains the four basic steps to a campaign of nonviolence. As you read aloud, ask students to note which of King's techniques are consistent with the strategies students listed on their anchor chart—and which ones aren't.

Quick-Think Pair Share. Students quickly share notes on their findings.

Pair Work. In paragraph 12, King talks about the pain of explaining injustice to a young child. Ask students to count off by twos and have them play out this parent–child scene in their new pair. Next, have them get with a new partner and reverse roles to ensure that students experience the dilemma from both perspectives.

- **Day 5**

Read Aloud. M. L. King's "Letter From Birmingham Jail": paragraphs 12–21

This section of the letter focuses on King's distinction between just and unjust laws.

Small-Group Work. First, ask students to summarize King's distinction between just and unjust laws. Then ask them to apply these distinctions to a series of modern laws—or rules within the school or the community, for example, locker searches or curfews.

Re-read. Have students re-read the end of paragraph 12, beginning with the sentence, "You express a great deal . . ."

OPINIONNAIRE SCALE FOR "LETTER FROM BIRMINGHAM JAIL"

When students have finished re-reading, ask them to place their personal viewpoint on the continuum on the following opinionnaire scale, a combination of an opinion-naire statement and a semantic differential scale (Figure 7.4).

Partner Work. Have students choose a partner whose views fall at least two scale points away from theirs. Partners discuss their views.

• Day 6

Reading. Assign students to read the remainder of M. L. King's "Letter From Birmingham Jail."

To increase transfer of knowledge and encourage independence, it's important to give students an opportunity to grapple with the text on their own. One great way to do so is to have students consciously apply different critical lenses in their reading (Chapter 4). Although the theories from which these lenses are derived are literary theories, we have found them equally useful to foster students' engaged attention on a wide variety of texts, including nonfiction.

OPINIONNAIRE SCALE FOR "LETTER FROM BIRMINGHAM JAIL"

NAME: ______________________ DATE: ____________

It is never okay to disobey a law.

One has a moral obligation to disobey an unjust law.

Available for download from **www.corwin.com/uncommoncore.**

Figure 7.4

READING "LETTER FROM BIRMINGHAM JAIL" THROUGH LITERARY LENSES: A GROUP ACTIVITY

Divide the class into five groups and assign each group one of the following literary lenses:

- Psychological
- Social power
- Formalist
- Historical
- Biographical

Part 1. Reading the Letter, One Lens at a Time

Each group receives the handout in Figure 7.5, which outlines the fundamental theoretical principles that undergird each lens and summarizes what those principles mean for reading and interpreting texts. Make certain that each group reads the description of the assigned lens and then discusses the following questions:

- What is this lens asking us to look at, to consider, when we read?
- Why is this perspective important in thinking about "Letter From Birmingham Jail?"
- If we apply this lens to "Letter From Birmingham Jail," the following passages stand out:
- If we apply this lens to this text, the following questions arise:
- We think this lens is/isn't (choose one) useful to reading letter because . . .

Part 2. The Jigsaw Move: Looking at the Letter Through Multiple Lenses

Regroup your class so that there is someone from each lens group in each new group. Then ask each new group to discuss the following questions:

- What was brought into sharper relief when you read the letter from your assigned lens?
- List some things that someone from a different group mentioned that never came up in your own lens discussion.
- Which lens or lenses seem to be the most useful in your analysis of "Letter From Birmingham Jail?" Why?

LITERARY PERSPECTIVES TOOLKIT

Literary perspectives help us explain why people might interpret the same text in a variety of ways. Perspectives help us understand what is important to individual readers, and they show us why those readers end up seeing what they see. One way to imagine a literary perspective is to think of it as a lens through which we can examine a text. No single lens gives us the clearest view, but it is sometimes fun to read a text with a particular perspective in mind because you often end up seeing something intriguing and unexpected. While readers typically apply more than one perspective at a time, the best way to understand these perspectives is to use them one at a time. What follows is a summary of some of the best-known literary perspectives. These descriptions are extremely brief, and none fully explains everything you might want to know about the perspective in question, but there is enough here for you to get an idea about how readers use them.

The Psychological Perspective

Some literary critics call this the psychological or character perspective because its purpose is to examine the internal motivations of literary characters. When we hear actors say that they are searching for their character's motivation, they are using something like this perspective. As a form of criticism, this perspective deals with works of literature as expressions of the personality, state of mind, feelings, and desires of the author or of a character within the literary work. As readers, we investigate the psychology of a character or an author to figure out the meaning of a text (although sometimes an examination of the author's psychology is considered biographical criticism, depending upon your point of view).

The Social Power Perspective

Some critics believe that human history and institutions, even our ways of thinking, are determined by the ways in which our societies are organized. Two primary factors shape our schemes of organization: economic power and social class membership. First, the class to which we belong determines our degree of economic, political, and social advantage, and so social classes invariably find themselves in conflict with each other. Second, our membership in a social class has a profound impact on our beliefs, values, perceptions, and our ways of thinking and feeling. For these reasons, the social power perspective helps us understand how people from different social classes understand the same circumstances in very different ways. When we see members of different social classes thrown together in the same story, we are likely to think in terms of power and advantage as we attempt to explain what happens and why.

The Formalist Perspective

The word "formal" has two related meanings, both of which apply within this perspective. The first relates to its root word, "form," a shape of structure that we can recognize and use to make associations. The second relates to a set

Figure 7.5

LITERARY PERSPECTIVES TOOLKIT (Continued)

of conventions or accepted practices. Formal poetry, for example, has meter, rhyme, stanza, and other predictable features that it shares with poems of the same type. The formalist perspective, then, pays particular attention to these issues of form and convention. Instead of looking at the world in which a poem exists, for example, the formalist perspective says that a poem should be treated as an independent and self-sufficient object. The methods used in this perspective are those of close reading: a detailed and subtle analysis of the formal components that make up the literary work, such as the meanings and interactions of words, figures of speech, and symbols.

The Historical Perspective

When applying this perspective you have to view a literary text within its historical context. Specific historical information will be of key interest: about the time during which an author wrote, about the time in which the text is set, about the ways in which people of the period saw and thought about the world in which they lived. History, in this case, refers to the social, political, economic, cultural, and/or intellectual climate of the time. For example, the literary works of William Faulkner frequently reflect the history of the American South, the Civil War and its aftermath, and the birth and death of a nation known as the Confederate States of America.

The Biographical Perspective

Because authors typically write about things they care deeply about and know well, the events and circumstances of their lives are often reflected in the literary works they create. For this reason, some readers use biographical information about an author to gain insight into that author's works. This lens, called biographical criticism, can be both helpful and dangerous. It can provide insight into themes, historical references, social oppositions or movements, and the creation of fictional characters. At the same time, it is not safe to assume that biographical details from the author's life can be transferred to a story or character that the author has created. For example, Ernest Hemingway and John Dos Passos were both ambulance drivers during World War I and both wrote novels about the war. Their experiences gave them firsthand knowledge and created strong personal feelings about the war, but their stories are still works of fiction. Some biographical details, in fact, may be completely irrelevant to the interpretation of that writer's work.

Here are some other lenses that can also be used as ways to consider texts. We won't be using them for our work with "Letter," but you will find them useful in your future reading.

Reader-Response Perspective

This type of perspective focuses on the activity of reading a work of literature. Reader-response critics turn away from the traditional idea that a literary work is an artifact that has meaning built within it; they turn their attention instead to the responses of individual readers. By this shift of perspective, a literary work is converted into an activity that goes on in a reader's mind. It is through this interaction that meaning is made. The features of the work itself—including narrator, plot, characters, style, and structure—are less important than the interplay between a reader's

LITERARY PERSPECTIVES TOOLKIT (Continued)

experience and the text. Advocates of this perspective believe that literature has no inherent or intrinsic meaning waiting to be discovered. Instead, meaning is constructed by readers as they bring their own thoughts, moods, and experiences to whatever text they are reading. In turn, what readers get out of a text depends upon their own expectations and ideas. For example, if you read "Sonny's Blues" by James Baldwin and you have your own troubled younger brother or sister, the story will have meaning for you that it wouldn't have for, say, an only child.

The Archetypal Perspective

In literary criticism, the word "archetype" signifies a recognizable pattern or a model. It can be used to describe story designs, character types, or images that can be found in a wide variety of works of literature. It can also be applied to myths, dreams, and social rituals. The archetypal similarities among texts and behaviors are thought to reflect a set of universal, even primitive ways of seeing the world. When we find them in literary works they evoke strong responses from readers. Archetypal themes include the heroic journey and the search for a father figure. Archetypal images include the opposition of paradise and Hades, the river as a sign of life and movement, and mountains or other high places as sources of enlightenment. Characters can be archetypal as well, like the rebel-hero, the scapegoat, the villain, and the goddess.

The Gender Perspective

Because gender is a way of viewing the world, people of different genders see things differently. For example, a feminist critic might see cultural and economic disparities as the products of a "patriarchal" society, shaped and dominated by men, who tend to decide things by various means of competition. Because women are frequently brought up to be more cooperative than competitive, they may find that such competition has hindered or prevented them from realizing their full potential, from turning their creative possibilities into action. In addition, societies often tend to see the male perspective as the default, that is, the one we choose automatically. As a result, women are identified is as the "other": the deviation or the contrasting type. When we use this lens, we examine patterns of thought, behavior, value, and power in relations between the sexes.

Deconstruction

Deconstruction is, at first, a difficult critical method to understand because it asks us to set aside ways of thinking that are quite natural and comfortable. For example, we frequently see the world as a set of opposing categories: male/female, rational/irrational, powerful/powerless. It also looks at the ways in which we assign value to one thing over another, such as life over death, presence over absence, and writing over speech. At its heart, deconstruction is a mode of analysis that asks us to question the very assumptions that we bring to that analysis. Gender, for example, is a "construct," a set of beliefs and assumptions that we have built, or constructed, over time and experience. But if we "de-construct" gender, looking at it while holding aside our internalized beliefs and expectations, new understandings become possible. To practice this perspective, then, we must constantly ask ourselves why we believe what we do about the make-up of our world and the ways in which we know it. Then, we must try to explain that world in the absence of our old beliefs.

Source: Reprinted by permission of the publisher. From Deborah Appleman, *Critical Encounters in High School English: Teaching Literary Theory to Adolescents, Second Edition,* New York: Teachers College Press. Copyright © 2009 by Teachers College, Columbia University. All rights reserved.

Available for download from **www.corwin.com/uncommoncore**.

Re-Read and Apply Theories. Students silently re-read the "Letter," applying the critical lens they were assigned. Ask them to identify five passages that stand out to them as they read it through their assigned lens.

Paragraph	Passage

After completing their charts on their own, students convene with their lens-alike groups to discuss the following questions:

- What elements of King's "Letter" seem especially important from the perspective of your lens?
- Based on your lens, what would you say is the overall theme or meaning you discovered in King's Letter?

• Day 7

Students briefly reconvene with their theory groups from the previous class meeting to conclude their discussion. Then, they reassemble into jigsaw groups.

Jigsaw Groups. Students work in jigsaw groups (i.e., each group contains members who examined *different* lenses) to share what they found. Groups discuss how each lens helped determine a different interpretation of the letter, bringing certain elements of the text into sharper relief.

Whole-Class Concluding Discussion. After the jigsaw sharing, have the whole class discuss the following questions:

- Which lenses seemed to work best with this text?

- What kinds of details did different lenses help you notice?

- How did the overall meaning of the letter change with each lens? Or did it?

- How can looking through multiple lenses enrich our understanding of "Letter From Birmingham Jail"?

CULMINATING PROJECTS

As you may recall, we argued earlier that building an inquiry unit requires planning backward from what kids will be doing as culminating projects and suggested that units

should include both a conventionally academic product and some other form of meaningful making.

Academic Project

Ask students to write a formal academic argument in which they identify an instance in which someone's rights are begin violated in their school or community and propose a plan of action that could be undertaken to rectify the situation. We suggest asking them write two versions of their arguments, one to their classmates and the other to someone whose actions or inattention somehow contributes to the problem.

Why two audiences? Remember, Coleman explained that whenever we read arguments, we construct both the arguments themselves and the arguments against which they are directed. That was our focal reading strategy for the unit. A complementary focal writing strategy is one articulated in the Standards themselves: adjusting one's arguments on the basis of "the audience's knowledge level, concerns, values, and possible biases" (National Governors Association Center for Best Practices/Council of Chief State School Officers, 2010a, p. 45), a strategy that can be best assessed when students are writing for real and different audiences.

After a consideration of the problems students identified, the class then chooses one on which they would work together in a social action project.

Social Action Project

Below are brief descriptions of five culminating social action projects designed by Jeff and Jeff's teachers reflecting their desired purpose and outcomes as expressed at the start of the unit. We think these are all solid and even inspiring projects.

- Emily Morgan's ninth-grade class engaged in a project to mentor refugee students in her school; the class is also teaching students to be mentors for students in lower grades.

- Amanda Micheletty's ninth graders trained to be peer tutors in their writing center and are creating video and written guides about how to survive and thrive in the high school environment.

- Angela Housley's fifth-grade class engaged in creating what they call "friendship cards" that give advice on how to disagree nicely, how to see and represent another's interest or rights, be strong when your rights are assailed, express reasonable expectations, work toward realizable and sustainable changes in the classroom and on the playground, and much else. The students use these as trading cards, and an archival copy of all the cards is in the counselor's office, to which she points students as a reference for navigating civil rights issues.

- Sam Mora's sophomores involved themselves in a bridge program to integrate refugee students into the school and to help them tell their stories and articulate their challenges. The group is hosting what they are calling cultural banquets during lunch at school to provide a context for interaction with refugee students and to allow the sharing of culture.

- Jeff had his high school students create quick video biographies of the refugee students in his class so that their stories and challenges can be shared. He challenged the students to do something to promote the natural human rights of classmates who face challenges.

But we want to point out that the outcome of the papers themselves and the social action projects hinge on students' having a deep understanding of civil rights and the range of ways people throughout history have dealt with the powers that be to promote those rights. A unit like the one outlined here can promote this deep understanding.

A Summary of This Unit's Approaches

We believe much more would be achieved in this kind of unit than in a Colemanesque close reading of the "Letter." With our approach, students would read the letter in its historical context but would read it as more than a historical document. They would read it as a document that helps them grapple with a question that's compelling in the here and now, one that could inform their thinking about how to work for change in the microculture of their lives, the mesoculture of their classroom and school, and in the macroculture of American culture and the world. The essential question, the frontloading, the sequencing of texts and activities, and the repeated practice with strategies necessary to be successful on the culminating projects not only cultivate interest and assist students in the more powerful use of literacy strategies, but also do something else: engage students in understanding both that they have the power to comprehend difficult texts and that they have the power to change themselves and the world around them.

Even as our instruction fosters this kind of engagement and understanding, it helps students develop the skills, strategies, perspectives, and habits of mind that will serve them well in their subsequent reading and schooling.

Principles of Practice

We hope that we have made it clear that we appreciate the need for standards. After all, how can you get where you want to go if you don't know where that destination happens to be? We believe that the CCSS have the capacity to foster increased attention to promoting deeper thinking and strategic facility as students engage with texts that others have written and compose their own.

The CCSS and whatever standards may replace them are part of the educational enterprise and can be allies in the adventure of teaching and learning. But they can't stand alone. Through the course of this book, we've worked to articulate *principles of practice* that will help teachers work toward those standards. Principles of practice constitute what cognitive scientists would call *heuristics*—flexible yet transferable tools for solving evolving problems and meeting challenges. Heuristics stand in stark contrast to algorithms or "one-size-fits-all" directives. Teaching and learning are too complex and too contextualized to be addressed through algorithms. That's why we need professional knowledge and the guidance of heuristic principles that can be flexibly adapted to new and changing situations.

After all, the world's only expert about what your students need and how to best teach them is *you*. Although standards can be powerful and principles of practice are necessary to professional teaching and problem solving, you must learn from your students how to best teach them. It has to be up to you what materials and methods will be best to leverage the kind of learning that will help them best meet the standards.

As we've talked to teachers about the CCSS as part of our work on this project, we've realized that many of the concerns we've heard are not about the CCSS themselves but about *what has been said about them*. We hope we've made it clear that David Coleman and his colleagues are not the Core. In fact, we think much of what they have said about the Core and how to implement it undermines the letter and spirit of the document itself.

Another common concern we've heard is also not about the CCSS themselves but rather about *how they are being implemented.* In many districts and states, teacher expertise and their independent professional decision making, foundational principles of the CCSS document, are being undercut by prescriptive curricula, materials, and implementation plans. If your district or state is mandating materials and methods in the name of the Core, then they are undermining the policy document itself and the legislation that put it into place. We hope that this book helps you speak against any initiatives that de-professionalize teaching and undermine the extent to which the CCSS can be a lever for progressive practice.

Of course, the CCSS themselves are not the only things that will influence teachers' practice. So too will the next generation of assessments. If our students are to be successful on those assessments, they will need the most powerful instruction possible.

After all, instruction is what has the single greatest impact on what students learn, master, and transfer (National Writing Project & Nagin, 2003). Powerful instruction is what we have focused on in this book. Standards are useful only to the degree that they empower and encourage, require and reward the most powerful instruction possible.

We're optimistic that this next generation of assessments can also be used as levers for progressive practice. These new assessments are designed not to test recall of information but rather to assess student mastery of strategies that make up the anchor standards. They will require actual reading and composing in "contexts of use" in both short and more extended performance tasks.

As this goes to press, several states are gearing up to have their students take a first pass at the next generation of tests. A couple of states have already done so. As expected, scores in these pilots were well below what they had been in the past. That's because the tests are significantly more challenging than past assessments and because proficiency has been redefined. Perhaps as a consequence, there is a lot of ink being spilled at

Many of the concerns we've heard from teachers are not about the CCSS themselves but about *what has been said about them* and *how they are being implemented.*

the moment about the tyranny of such tests and how teachers should resist them. We sympathize with this view to a certain degree and share many concerns, but we want to make several points.

1. The next generation of assessments, both in the United States and the rest of the world, are an improvement over most of what has been done in the past. For the most part, the short and long performance task items actually assess problem solving, situated strategy use, reading, and writing in ways that correspond to how experts use these processes in real life and in disciplinary work. Could the tests be better? For sure. But do the new tests represent significant progress? We think so. To take just one example, Idaho's previous test tested through multiple-choice questions rather than the complex writing performances the new tests will require.

2. The next generation of assessments in the United States align us more closely with more rigorous international assessments. This was one of the reasons for the Core in the first place and the reason it enjoyed widespread and bipartisan support (at least initially). We are now operating in an international context and are compared to schools and systems on an international basis. There is nowhere to hide.

3. For the foreseeable future, we are going to have high-stakes assessments and accountability for student learning. When Jonathan Kozol spoke recently as a Distinguished Speaker for Boise State University, Jeff was his driver. In one conversation, Kozol argued that, as civil servants, teachers are in the position of being "accountable" and "answerable"—that is, that we have to prove that what we do works. He argued both that there must be metrics and performances that the public understands and that it is part of our job to assess the assessments, to be advocates for how to improve them and for how they should be interpreted.

Accountability and Assessments

The desire for accountability means that for the foreseeable future, teachers are going to have to prepare students to meet the challenge of the new assessments. Therefore, powerful instruction is more important than ever before. Students are being asked on the tests (and therefore must be asked in school and at home) to read more, to read across different kinds of texts, to solve a problem with the data they have processed and then reflect and write about *how* they solved the problem. This means that students will need to learn how to activate what they already know so they can bring that knowledge to bear as resources for their reading. In this book, we have shown you multiple ways to do this.

Because students will be reading both more *different kinds* of texts and more *complex* texts for the new generation of assessments, we need to teach them how to transfer their learning from one textual context to another. As we have argued, transfer can be achieved only by cultivating a spirit of transfer by having students name and justify what they learn, apply it to new situations, reflect on that application, and consider future possible applications. As we have shown, text-dependent questions do not cultivate transfer. But instruction that is situated in inquiry contexts, that builds knowledge text by text and activity by activity, that provides meaningful practice until heuristics are mastered, and that requires continuous practice and development and application over time *does* do this.

The new assessments will ask students to demonstrate proficiency in complex tasks. Among other things, the next generation of assessments will ask students to do the following:

- **Put texts into conversation with each other.** Students will be asked to see complex implied relationships inside longer texts and across various texts and data sets. This means that we need to create sequences of instruction, situated in ongoing inquiries that give students practice doing just that. The emphasis the authors of the CCSS place on "this text and this text alone" doesn't do that. The instruction we talk about in this book does.

- **Foreground problem solving and use logical evidentiary reasoning to make cases and compose arguments.** This means that we need to create contexts that require, support, and reward these activities. We know from classroom research that New Critical classrooms result in little discussion, little accountable talk, little real argumentation and problem solving. The instruction that we suggest engages students in responding to authentic questions and real problems that will require that they hone their argumentative skills.

- **Include and create multimodal texts** in the forms of graphs, tables, data sets, photos, and the like in their writing and comprehend them in their reading. Text complexity as expressed in the lists of exemplar texts in Appendix B (NAGC Center/CCSSO, 2010b) privileges conventional texts, which is both at odds with the tests and with the Standards themselves. In this book, we try to demonstrate how to expand the range of texts you include in your classroom. Text complexity, as reflected in the lists in the CCSS document and its appendices is oversimplified to the detriment of students and teacher decision making. We encourage you to think about interpretive complexity in addition to text complexity to help students progress from their own current capacities to new levels of competence.

Final Thoughts

This political moment in time will pass. The Core will be revised or replaced. David Coleman will surely disappear from the scene. New assessments will evolve. But students and teachers, their relationships, and their relationships with texts and literacy will remain. Identifying and promoting good teaching will always be essential. Good teaching is not a fad; it cannot be politically dictated and cannot follow political trends.

> Good teaching is not a fad; it cannot be politically dictated and cannot follow political trends.

We can't let political tides and policies lead us to throw out what we know about best practice. We need to stand against what is arbitrary and uninformed. We must be wide-awake practitioners who are in touch with articulated principles of powerful practice and who are willing speak about them. But as we engage in this process, we need to remain open-minded inquirers into the possibilities of any reform and not resist them in knee-jerk fashion either.

We stand, as individual teachers and as a profession, at a moment in history. We hope this book is useful to you in this moment. We hope it helps you stand against bad ideas and stand up for good ones. We hope it helps you achieve the promise of the CCSS and avoid the pitfalls. We hope it helps you get it right for your students both now and in the future.

References

Achieve the Core. (2013). A close reading of Lincoln's "Gettysburg Address." Retrieved from http://www.achievethecore.org/page/35/the-gettysburg-address -by-abraham-lincoln

Allington, R. L., & Cunningham, P. M. (2010). Prior knowledge plays a large role in reading comprehension. Retrieved from http://www.education.com/reference/ article/prior-knowledge-reading-comprehension

Anagnostopoulos, D. M. (2000). *Setting standards, failing students: A case study of merit promotion in two Chicago high schools* (Unpublished doctoral dissertation). University of Chicago, Chicago, IL.

Anderson, R. C., & Pearson, P. D. (1984). A schema-theoretic view of basic processes in reading. In P. D. Pearson (Ed.), *Handbook of reading research* (pp. 255–291). New York, NY: Longman.

Applebee, A. N. (1993). *Literature in the secondary school: Studies of curriculum and instruction in the United States.* Urbana, IL: National Council of Teachers of English.

Applebee, A. N., Burroughs, R., & Stevens, A. (2000). Creating continuity and coherence in high school literature curricula. *Research in the Teaching of English, 34,* 396–428.

Applebee, A. N., Langer, J. A., Nystrand, M., & Gamoran, A. (2003). Discussion-based approaches to developing understanding: Classroom instruction and student performance in middle and high school English. *American Educational Research Journal, 40,* 685–730.

Appleman, D. (2006). *Reading for themselves: How to transform adolescents into lifelong readers through out-of-class book clubs.* Portsmouth, NH: Heinemann.

Appleman, D. (2009). *Critical encounters in high school English: Teaching literary theory to adolescents* (2nd ed.). New York, NY: Teachers College Press.

Appleman, D. (2010). *Adolescent literacy and the teaching of reading: Lessons for teachers of literature.* Urbana, IL: National Council of Teachers of English.

Appleman, D., & Graves, M. (2012). *Reading better, reading smarter: Designing literature lessons for adolescents.* Portsmouth, NH: Heinemann.

Bancroft, C., & Rabinowitz, P. (2013). Euclid at the Core: Recentering literary education. *Style, 48*(1), 1–34.

Beach, R. (1993). *A teacher's introduction to reader-response theories.* Urbana, IL: National Council of Teachers of English.

Beers, K., & Probst, R. E. (2013). *Notice & note: Strategies for close reading.* Portsmouth, NH: Heinemann.

Biancarosa, C., & Snow, C. (2006). *Reading next—A vision for action and research in middle and high school literacy: A report to the Carnegie Corporation of New York* (2nd ed.). Washington, DC: Alliance for Excellent Education.

Black, P., & William, D. (1998). Inside the black box: Raising standards through classroom assessment. *Phi Delta Kappan, 80*(2), 139–148.

Bloom, B. (Ed.). (1956). *Taxonomy of educational objectives: The classification of educational objectives. Handbook I cognitive domain.* New York: Longman.

Booth, W. (1974). *A rhetoric of irony.* Chicago, IL: University of Chicago Press.

Bransford, J. D., & Johnson, M. K. (1972). Contextual prerequisites for understanding: Some investigations of comprehension and recall. *Journal of Verbal Learning and Verbal Behavior, 11, 717–726.*

Brown, J., Collins, A., & DuGuid, P. (1989). Situated cognition and the culture of learning. *Educational Researcher, 18*(1), 32–42.

Bruner, J. S. (1966). *Toward a theory of instruction,* Cambridge, MA: Belknap Press.

Byrnes, J. P. (2008). *Cognitive development and learning in instructional contexts* (3rd ed.). New York, NY: Allyn & Bacon.

Church, G. (1997). The significance of Louise Rosenblatt on the field of teaching literature. *Inquiry, 1,* 71–77.

Close reading of text: "Letter From Birmingham Jail," Martin Luther King, Jr. [Video]. (2011). New York, NY: EngageNY. Retrieved from http://vimeo.com/27056255

Coleman, D. (2011, April 28). *Bringing the common core to life.* Presentation to New York State Department of Education, Albany, NY. Retrieved from http://usny .nysed.gov/rttt/docs/bringingthecommoncoretolife/fulltranscript.pdf

Coleman, D., & Pimentel, S. (2012). *Revised publishers' criteria for the Common Core State Standards in English language arts and literacy, grades 3–12.* Retrieved from http://www.corestandards.org/assets/Publishers_Criteria_for_3-12.pdf

Common Core in ELA/literacy: Shift 4: Text-based answers [Video]. (2012, October 30). New York, NY: EngageNY. Retrieved from http://www.engageny.org/ resource/common-core-in-ela-literacy-shift-4-text-based-answers

Connolly, W., & Smith, M. W. (2003). Dropping in a mouse: Reading poetry with our students. *The Clearing House, 76,* 235–240.

Cunningham, G. (2009). Lesson plans and unit plans: The basis for instruction. In B. Cunningham, *The new teacher's companion: Practical wisdom for succeeding in the classroom* (pp. 103–127). Alexandria, VA: ASCD. Retrieved from http://www.ascd.org/publications/books/109051/chapters/Lesson-Plans-and-Unit-Plans@-The-Basis-for-Instruction.aspx

Cunningham, J. (2013). Research on text complexity: The Common Core State Standards as catalyst. In S. Neuman & L. Gambrell (Eds.), *Quality reading instruction in the age of common core standards* (pp. 136–148). Newark, DE: International Reading Association.

Damasio, A. (2005). *Descartes' error.* New York, NY: Penguin.

Dawson, P. (2005, January). Sleep and adolescents. *Principal Leadership.* Retrieved from http://www.nasponline.org/resources/principals/sleep%20disorders%20web.pdf

Discussion of the Common Core State Standards for English Language Arts & Literacy and "Letter From Birmingham Jail" by Dr. Martin Luther King [Video]. (2011, June 20). Retrieved from http://neric.welearntube.org/?q=node/147

Doidge, N. (2007). *The brain that changes itself.* New York: Penguin.

Dooling, D. J., & Lachman, R. (1971). Effects of comprehension on retention of prose. *Journal of Experimental Psychology, 88,* 216–222.

Dykstra, D. (2006). Testimony to education at the Idaho State Legislature, Education Committee of the House of Representatives, April 3, 2006. Retrieved from http://www.ipn.uni-kiel.de/aktuell/stcse/stcse.html

Elizabeth, T., Ross Anderson, T. L., Snow, E. H., & Selman, R. (2012). Academic discussions: An analysis of instructional discourse and an argument for an integrative assessment framework. *American Educational Research Journal, 49,* 1214–1250.

Ericsson, K. A., & Lehmann, C. (1996). Expert and exceptional performance: Evidence of maximal adaptation to task constraints. *Annual Review of Psychology, 47,* 273–305. doi:10.1146/annurev.psych.47.1.273

Fellner, J. (2013, August 19). Graying prisoners. *New York Times,* A19.

FitzPatrick, D. (2005). Reading level response: Helping students write about literature. In T. McCann, L. R. Johannesson, E. Kahn, P. Smagorinsky, & M. W. Smith (Eds.), *Reflective teaching, reflective learning: How to develop critically engaged readers, writers, and speakers* (pp. 147–165). Portsmouth, NH: Heinemann.

Fredricksen, J., Wilhelm, J., & Smith, M. (2012). *So what's the story?* Portsmouth, NH: Heinemann.

The Gettysburg Address: An exemplary curricular module in literacy [Video.] (2011). Retrieved from http://www.pbslearningmedia.org/resource/engny.pd.ccvs .ela9/the-gettysburg-address-an-exemplary-curricular-module-in-literacy

Gladwell, M. (2008). *Outliers.* New York, NY: Little, Brown.

Gladwell, M. (2013). *David and Goliath: Underdogs, misfits, and the art of battling giants.* New York, NY: Little, Brown.

Goldman, S. (2012). Adolescent literacy: Learning and understanding content. *Future Child, 22*(2), 89–116.

Graff, G. (1989). *Professing literature.* Chicago, IL: University of Chicago Press.

Guthrie, J. T., Klauda, S. L., & Morrison, D. A. (2012). Motivation, achievement, and classroom contexts for information book reading. In J. T Guthrie, A. Wigfield, A., & S. L. Klauda (Eds.), *Adolescents' engagement in academic literacy* (Report No. 7, pp. 1–51). Retrieved from http://www.cori.umd.edu/ research-publications/2012_adolescents_engagement_ebook.pdf

Haft, S., Witt, P. J., Thomas, T. (Producers), & Weir, P. (Director). (1989). *Dead poets society* [Motion picture]. United States: Touchstone Pictures.

Haidt, J. (2006). *The happiness hypothesis.* New York: Basic Books.

Haskell, R. (2000). *Transfer of learning: Cognition, instruction, and reasoning.* San Diego, CA: Academic Press.

Hill, M. L. (2009). *Beats, rhymes and classroom life: Hip-hop pedagogy and the politics of identity.* New York, NY: Teachers College Press.

Hillocks, G. Jr. (1986). *Research on written composition: New directions for teaching.* Urbana, IL: ERIC and National Conference for Research in English.

Hillocks, G., Jr. (1995). *Teaching writing as reflective practice.* New York, NY: Teachers College Press.

Hillocks, G., Jr. (2011). *Teaching argument writing, grades 6–12: Supporting claims with relevant evidence and clear reasoning.* Portsmouth, NH: Heinemann.

Hillocks, G., Jr., & Ludlow, L. (1984). A taxonomy of skills in reading and interpreting fiction. *American Educational Research Journal, 21,* 7–24.

Hillocks, G., Jr., McCabe, B., & McCampbell, J. F. (1971). *The dynamics of English instruction.* New York, NY: Random House.

Hillocks, G., & Smith, M. W. (1988). Sensible sequencing: Developing knowledge about literature text by text. *English Journal, 96,* 44–49.

Hollander, C. N. (2013, June 8). No learning without feeling. *New York Times.* Retrieved from www.nytimes.com/2013/06/09/opinion/sunday/no-learning-without-feeling.html

Hughes, L. (1990). Harlem. In *Selected poems of Langston Hughes.* Retrieved from http://www.poetryfoundation.org/poem/175884

Krathwohl, D. R. (2002). A revision of Bloom's taxonomy: An overview. *Theory Into Practice, 4,* 212–218.

Lakoff, G. (2008). *The political mind.* New York, NY: Penguin.

Langer, J. A. (2001). Beating the odds: Teaching middle and high school students to read and write well. *American Educational Research Journal, 38,* 837–880.

Lanser, S. (1981). *The narrative act: Point of view in prose fiction.* Princeton, NJ: Princeton University Press.

Lee, L. Y. (1986). The gift. In *Rose.* Retrieved from http://www.poetryfoundation.org/poem/171752

Marcotte, D., & Hansen, B. (2010). Time for school. *Education Next, 10*(1), 53–59. Retrieved from http://educationnext.org/time-for-school

Marshall, J. (1991). Writing and reasoning about literature. In R. Beach & S. Hynds (Eds.), *Developing discourse practices in adolescence and adulthood* (pp. 161–180). Norwood, NJ: Ablex.

McCann, T., Johannessen, L. R., Kahn, E., & Flanagan, J. M. (2006). *Talking in class: Using discussion to enhance teaching and learning.* Urbana, IL: National Council of Teachers of English.

MacLennan, C. (2012, August 20). What's missing from the Common Core? [Blog post]. Retrieved from http://www.devstu.org/blogs/what-s-missing-from-the-common-core-state-standards

Middle school ELA curriculum video: Close reading of a text: MLK "Letter From Birmingham Jail" [Video]. (2012, December 5). New York, NY: EngageNY. Retrieved from http://www.engageny.org/resource/middle-school-ela-curriculum-video-close-reading-of-a-text-mlk-letter-from-birmingham-jail

Morrell, E. (2002). Toward a critical pedagogy of popular culture: Literacy development among urban youth. *Journal of Adolescent and Adult Literacy, 46*, 72–77.

National Governors Association Center for Best Practices/Council of Chief State School Officers. (2010a). *Common core state standards for English language arts & literacy in history/social studies, science, and technical subjects.* Retrieved from http://www.corestandards.org/wp-content/uploads/ELA_Standards.pdf

National Governors Association Center for Best Practices/Council of Chief State School Officers. (2010b). *Common core state standards for English language arts & literacy in history/social studies, science, and technical subjects. Appendix B: Text exemplars and sample performance tasks.* Retrieved from http://www.corestandards.org/assets/Appendix_B.pdf

National Governors Association Center for Best Practices/Council of Chief State School Officers. (2012). *Common core state standards initiative: English language arts standards—Resources—Key points in English language arts.* Retrieved from http://www.corestandards.org/resources/key-points-in-english-language-arts

National Writing Project & Nagin, C. (2003). *Because writing matters: Improving student writing in our schools.* San Francisco, CA: Jossey Bass.

New London Group. (1996). A pedagogy of multiliteracies: Designing social futures. *Harvard Educational Review, 66*(1), 60–92.

Newkirk, T. (2013). *Speaking back to the Common Core.* Portsmouth, NH: Heinemann. Retrieved from http://heinemann.com/shared/onlineresources%5CE02123%5CNewkirk_Speaking_Back_to_the_Common_Core.pdf

Newman, F., & Associates. (1996). *Authentic achievement: Restructuring of schools for intellectual quality.* San Francisco, CA: Jossey-Bass.

Newman, F., & Wehlage, G. (1995). *Successful school restructuring: A report to the public and educators by the Center on Organization and Restructuring of Schools.* Madison: Board of Regents of the University of Wisconsin System and Document service, Wisconsin Center for Education Research.

Nystrand, M., with Gamoran, A., Kachur, R., & Prendergast, C. (1997). *Opening dialogue: Understanding the dynamics of language and learning in the English classroom.* New York, NY: Teachers College Press.

Overturf, B. (2011). Common Core: Seven opportunities to transform English language arts curriculum [Blog post comment]. Retrieved from http://www.edutopia.org/blog/common-core-state-standards-2-virginia-goatley?page=16

Parker, S. (2013, May 14). Strange political bedfellows join forces against the Common Core. *TakePart.* Retrieved from http://www.takepart.com/article/2013/05/14/common-core-standards-progressives-conservatives-against

Perkins, D., & Salomon, G. (1988). Teaching for transfer. *Educational Leadership, 46*(1), 22–32.

Pirie, B. (1997). Beyond Barney and the cult of the individual. In *Reshaping high school English* (pp. 8–16). Urbana, IL: National Council of Teachers of English.

Porter, A., McMaken, J., Hwang, J., & Yang, R. (2011). Common Core Standards: The new U.S. intended curriculum. *Educational Researcher, 40*,103–116.

Porter-Magee, K. (2012). How will reading instruction change when aligned to the Common Core? *Common Core Watch*. Retrieved from http://www.edexcellence.net/commentary/education-gadfly-daily/common-core-watch/2012/how-will-reading-instruction-change-when-aligned-to-the-common-core.html

Rabinowitz, P. (1987). *Before reading*. Ithaca, NY: Cornell University Press.

Rabinowitz, P. J. (1993). "Reader, I blew him away": Convention and transgression in Sue Grafton. In A. Booth (Ed.), *Famous last words: Changes in gender and narrative closure* (pp. 326–346). Charlottesville: University Press of Virginia.

Rabinowitz, P., & Smith, M. W. (1998). *Authorizing readers: Resistance and respect in the teaching of literature*. New York, NY: Teachers College Press.

Radway, J. (1984). *Reading the romance: Women, patriarchy, and popular literature*. Chapel Hill: University of North Carolina Press.

Raphael, T. E. (1982). Question-answering strategies for children. *The Reading Teacher, 36,* 186–190.

Ravitch, D. (2013, February 26). Why I cannot support the Common Core Standards [Blog post]. http://dianeravitch.net/2013/02/26/why-i-cannot-support-the-common-core-standards

Rex, L., & McEachen, D. (1999). "If anything is odd, inappropriate, confusing, or boring, it's probably important": The emergence of inclusive academic literacy through English classroom discussion practices. *Research in the Teaching of English, 34,* 65–129.

Richards, I. A. (1929). *Practical criticism: A study of literary judgment*. Edinburgh, Scotland: Edinburgh Press.

Rosenblatt, L. (1938). *Literature as exploration*. New York, NY: Appleton-Century.

Scholes, R. (2001). *The crafty reader*. New Haven, CT: Yale University Press.

Science Media Group. (1989). *A private universe*. Cambridge, MA: Harvard University, Smithsonian Institution.

Short, K. (2013, January 7). Common Core State Standards: Misconceptions about exemplars [Blog post]. Retrieved from http://wowlit.org/blog/2013/01/07/common-core-state-standards-misconceptions-about-text-exemplars

Sitomer, A. (2012, February 9). Common Core: The David Coleman dilemma [Blog post]. Retrieved from http://www.alanlawrencesitomer.com/2012/02/09/3254-common-core-the-david-coleman-dilemma

Smith, M. W. (1991). *Understanding unreliable narrators: Reading between the lines in the literature classroom*. Urbana, IL: National Council of Teachers of English.

Smith, M. W., & Wilhelm. J. (2002). *"Reading don't fix no Chevys": Literacy in the lives of young men*. Portsmouth, NH: Heinemann.

Smith, M. W., & Wilhelm, J. (2006). *Going with the flow: How to engage boys (and girls) in their literacy learning*. Portsmouth, NH: Heinemann.

Smith, M. W., & Wilhelm, J. (2010). *Fresh takes on teaching literary elements: How to teach what really matters about character, setting, point of view, and theme*. New York, NY: Scholastic.

Smith, M. W., Wilhelm, J., & Fredricksen, J. (2012). *Oh Yeah? Teaching argument to meet and exceed the CCSS*. Portsmouth, NH: Heinemann.

Tharp, R. G., & Gallimore, R. (1988). *Rousing minds to life: Teaching, learning, and schooling in social context.* New York, NY: Cambridge University Press.

Thomas, P. L. (2013, December 23). This is the Common Core you support? [Blog post]. Retrieved from http://atthechalkface.com/2013/12/23/this-is-the-common-core-you-support

Tyson, L. (2006). *Critical theory today: A user friendly guide* (2nd ed.). New York, NY: Routledge.

Varlas, L. (2012). It's complicated: Common Core State Standards focus on text complexity. *Education Update, 54*(4). Retrieved from http://www.ascd.org/publications/newsletters/education-update/apr12/vol54/num04/It's-Complicated.aspx

Vygotsky, L. S. (1978). *Mind in society: The development of higher psychological processes.* Cambridge, MA: Harvard University Press.

White, D. (1993). Effects of autobiographical writing before reading on students' responses to short stories. *Journal of Educational Research, 88,* 173–184.

Wieman, C. (2005, July). *Learning physics through inquiry.* Keynote for Southern Colorado Literacy Conference, Pueblo, CO.

Wiggins, G. (2013, May 1). The Common Core Standards: A defense [Blog post]. Retrieved from http://grantwiggins.wordpress.com/2013/05/01/the-common-core-standards-a-defense

Wilhelm, J. 2002). *Action strategies for deepening comprehension: Using drama strategies to assist improved reading performance.* New York, NY: Scholastic.

Wilhelm, J. (2007). *Engaging readers and writers with inquiry.* New York, NY: Scholastic.

Wilhelm, J. (2008). *You gotta be the book: Teaching engaged and reflective reading with adolescents* (2nd ed.). New York: Teachers College Press.

Wilhelm, J. (2012a). *Action strategies for deepening comprehension.* New York: Scholastic.

Wilhelm, J. (2012b). *Enriching comprehension with visualization* (2nd ed.). New York, NY: Scholastic.

Wilhelm, J. (2012c). *Improving comprehension with think alouds.* New York, NY: Scholastic.

Wilhelm, J., Baker, T., & Dube, J. (2001). *Strategic reading.* Portsmouth, NH: Heinemann.

Wilhelm, J., & Novak, B. (2011). *Teaching literacy for love and wisdom: Being the book and being the change.* New York, NY: Teachers College Press.

Wilhelm, J., & Smith, M. W. (2014). *Reading unbound: Why kids need to read what they want—and why we should let them.* New York, NY: Scholastic.

Wilhelm, J., Wilhelm, P., & Boas, E. (2009). *Inquiring minds learn to read and write.* Oakville, Ontario, Canada: Rubicon.

Wittgenstein, L. (1953/2001). *Philosophical investigations* (3rd ed., G. E. M. Anscombe, Trans.). Malden, MA: Blackwell.

Zavitovsky, P. (2012, March 12). Testing and the Common Core. *Catalyst Chicago.* Retrieved from http://www.catalyst-chicago.org/news/2012/03/19/19935/testing-and-common-core

Index

CORWIN LITERACY

Harvey "Smokey" Daniels & Elaine Daniels

On that single method for transforming students from passive spectators into active learners

Nancy Frey & Douglas Fisher

On five access points for seriously stretching students' capacity to comprehend complex text

Nancy Boyles

On classroom-ready resources to get close reading right in grades 3–6

Gretchen Bernabei & Judi Reimer

On 101 lessons and mentor texts for tackling the most persistent issues in academic writing

Sara Holbrook & Michael Salinger

On how to teach today's i-touch generation precision writing and reading in any subject

Kathy Barclay & Laura Stewart

On best texts and practices for teaching informational reading to young kids

BECAUSE ALL TEACHERS ARE LEADERS

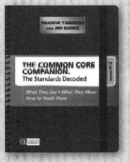

Sharon Taberski

On that grades K–2 *Companion* teachers have been pleading for

Leslie Blauman

On the how-to's of putting the grades 3–5 standards into day-to-day practice

Jim Burke

On what the 6–8 standards really say, really mean, and how to put them into practice

Jim Burke

On that version of the 9–12 standards all high school teachers wish they had

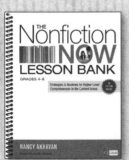

Nancy Akhavan

On top-notch nonfiction lessons and texts for maximizing students' content-area understanding

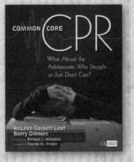

ReLeah Lent & Barry Gilmore

On practical strategies for coaxing our most resistant learners into engagement and achievement

N141E3-E

CORWIN

A SAGE Company

The Corwin logo—a raven striding across an open book— represents the union of courage and learning. Corwin is committed to improving education for all learners by publishing books and other professional development resources for those serving the field of PreK–12 education. By providing practical, hands-on materials, Corwin continues to carry out the promise of its motto: **"Helping Educators Do Their Work Better."**